CW01669889

Shakespeare and Cognition

Aristotle's Legacy and Shakespearean Drama

Arthur F. Kinney

Routledge
Taylor & Francis Group
New York London

Routledge is an imprint of the
Taylor & Francis Group, an informa business

Routledge
Taylor & Francis Group
270 Madison Avenue
New York, NY 10016

Routledge
Taylor & Francis Group
2 Park Square
Milton Park, Abingdon
Oxon OX14 4RN

Routledge is an imprint of Taylor & Francis Group, an Informa business

Printed in the United States of America on acid-free paper
10 9 8 7 6 5 4 3 2 1

International Standard Book Number-10: 0-415-97753-3 (Softcover) 0-415-97752-5 (Hardcover)
International Standard Book Number-13: 978-0-415-97753-1 (Softcover) 978-0-415-97752-4 (Hardcover)

Library of Congress Cataloging-in-Publication Data

Kinney, Arthur F., 1933-
Shakespeare and cognition : Aristotle's legacy and Shakespearean drama / Arthur F. Kinney.
p. cm.
Includes bibliographical references and index.
ISBN 0-415-97752-5 (hb) -- ISBN 0-415-97753-3 (pb)
1. Shakespeare, William, 1564-1616--Criticism and interpretation. 2. Shakespeare, William, 1564-1616--Philosophy. 3. Shakespeare, William, 1564-1616--Knowledge--Psychology. 4. Aristotle--Influence. 5. Cognition in literature. I. Title.

PR3001.K55 2006
822.3'3--dc22 2005035559

Visit the Taylor & Francis Web site at
http://www.taylorandfrancis.com

and the Routledge Web site at
http://www.routledge-ny.com

Shakespeare and Cognition

CONTENTS

The raison d'être of poetics is to make explicit and rational, and to test the coherence of, the theories that enable interpretation to take place.

Peter Brooks

Goats graze on bitter herbs and make sweet milk of it, and from the selfsame flower do honey bees derive their sweet honey and spiders their deadly poisons.

Johannes Reuchlin

No ideas but in things.

William Carlos Williams

Dedication

For my Australian colleagues

and

in memory of Lloyd Davis,
Herbert Berry, and Scott McMillin

LIST OF ILLUSTRATIONS

PREFACE

At the initial meeting of his playing company of mechanicals in *A Midsummer Night's Dream*, the carpenter Peter Quince distributes parts and then gives to himself the most fundamental part of all: "I will draw a bill of properties," he tells them, "much as our play wants" (1.2.105–06).[1] He knows that members of the Athenian court, like playgoers at Shakespeare's Globe, go to see a play as much or more than to hear it, although he is unlikely aware that the original Greek root of theater is *theasthai* (to watch). Shakespeare's Lucrece makes explicit what Peter Quince implies. "Out, idle words, servants to shallow fools, Unprofitable wounds, weak arbitrators!" she cries; "To see sad sights," comments the poet, "moves more than hear them told" (*The Rape of Lucrece*, 1016–17; 1324). Shakespeare's audiences seem to have agreed. Samuel Rowlands commented on the constant attention Richard Burbage paid his dagger when performing Richard III in Shakespeare's time. Simon Forman remembered the chair in *Macbeth*, the bracelet and chest in *Cymbeline*, and Autolycus' pack in *The Winter's Tale*.[2] "The joint-stool in *Macbeth*, "James Calderwood writes, changes "from an object in the Globe Theater to an object in Macbeth's castle to the hallucinated ghost of Banquo."[3]

Stage properties can hold the same fascination and dominance for us today, endowed with magical, ritual, historical or cultural meanings. A skull can remind us of Hamlet, a dagger of Brutus, a bed of Desdemona, an asp of Cleopatra. Indeed, stage properties were sufficiently valuable to cause Robert Davies to sign certain Articles when joining Lady Elizabeth's Men in 1614 that penalized taking properties outside the theater.[4] In assessing such plays, Thomas Heywood writes in *An Apology of Actors* in 1612 that "Playes are in use as they are understood,

Spectators eyes may make them bad or good."[5] Stephen Gosson had similar thoughts, but he narrowed the probable options and feared the results. "Sometime you shall see nothing but the aduentures of an amorous knight, passing from countrie to countrie for the loue of his lady, encōtring many a terible monster made of broune paper, & at his retorne, is so wonderfully changed, that he can not be knowne but by some posie in his tablet, or by a broken ring, or a handkircher, or a piece of cockle shell, what learne you by that?" he argues in *Playes Confuted in Fiue Actions* (1582); "delight beeing moued with varietie of shewes, of euentes, or musicke, the longer we gaze, that more we craue, yea so forcible they are [that] afterwards being but thought vpō, they make vs seeke for the like an other time" (sigs. C6, F6) — in apparent agreement with Thomas Rymer, who later complains of such properties as "clutter" (*A Short View of Tragedy* [1693], p. 135). This drama is spectacular.

Such observations agree with Aristotle's pronouncement that sight is man's primary way of understanding, the most important of his five senses. The eye perceives objects through patterns of reflected light that enter the eyes through the pupils, are gathered by the lens, and thrown onto the retina, a screen at the back of the eyes. The retina in turn acts as a network of nerve fibers that passes light and color, sending such information along circuits to the brain, where it is interpreted. Here, however, perceptions differ from individual to individual, depending on how the raw data is combined with past experiences, cultural conventions, and personal memory to form the basis for meaning. Interpretations can vary widely, despite a common source in what is being seen; at other times, distinctions can be tiny ones. In either case, "as soon as we experience something" of our own particular neural pathways, worn over time by related visual experiences, we "immediately interpret it and rewire it," as John J. Ratney has it.[6] This subsequent processing was recognized in the early modern period, not just in our own, as in "A dialog betweene the auctour and his eye" added to Richard Edwards' 1578 edition of his *Paradyse of Dainty Deuises*:

Auctour: My eye why didst thou light on that, which was not thyne?
Why hast thou with thy sight, thus slaine an harte of myne?
O thou unhappie eye, would God thou hadst been blinde,
When first thou didst her spie, for whom this grief I finde.

Eye: Why sir it is not I, that doe deserue suche blame,
Your fancie not your eye, is causer of the same.
For I am readie prest, as page that serues your ease,
To searche what thyng is beste, that might your fancie please.[7]

In looking at a play, then, and in looking especially at stage properties as I intend — physical objects that contribute to signification and meaning in drama — we employ sight and mind individually in order to understand and to relay meaning. Playgoing is a matter of cognition — that is, how human beings acquire and process information. In each one of us, Rita Carter writes, "The brain is full of prejudices: habits of thought, knee-jerk emotional reactions and automatic orderings of perception. These are so deeply ingrained that we are usually unaware that they exist, and when we become aware of them we think of them as common sense assumptions or intuition."[8] Our brains work just as those of the Elizabethans worked, genetically, experientially, and culturally, and, like them, we often see not what we are looking at but rather what we want to see or what we have been trained to see. At the same time — even at the same performance — each of us now as then might see different things.

Such interior distinctions are supplemented by exterior conditioning to form individual interpretative frames. None of us sees a play from exactly the same place or the same position as someone else, and this difference is recorded on the retina. No single spectator ever sees an object, a stage property, precisely the way someone else does. Social forces, too — what Edward Said once called "social density"[9] — affect each person differently. The evolution of thought by comparison with past experiences, a fundamental operation of the brain, is unique. We view plays, as spectators, along what Jacques Derrida, in *Of Grammatology* (1967) in somewhat different contexts, called "corridors of meaning" — that is, related perceptions a person builds up over time without the complicity of an author.[10] And just because of such contexts — those of the moment the play was written, those of performance, and those of sight — stage spectacles and stage properties may change from viewing to viewing, either from performance to performance or from an appearance at one moment in a play to a reappearance later on. Thus, to see a bed in a performance may suggest lust, seduction, nuptials, or consummation; it may be the bed that Desdemona uses to win back Othello or the bed on which the dying King Henry IV finds himself betrayed by a son who prematurely takes up his crown, or, as in the instance of Mariana's bed in *Measure for Measure*, a stage property vital to the plot that is never seen at all. Such vital stage properties — the hawthorn brake in *A Midsummer Night's Dream* is another — are seen not by the eye but, rather, in the mind's eye, as "store[d] up, as [in] a triple eye," as Helena suggests to the King of France in *All's Well That Ends Well* (2.1.108). It is in the mind's eye that Henry V visualizes the potential horrors at Harfleur, that Rosaline sees herself with "A gallant curtle-axe upon my thigh,

A boar-spear in my hand" (*As You Like It*, 1.2.117–18), that Leontes perceives Hermione's adultery with Polixenes and his son Mamillius as a bastard (*The Winter's Tale*, 1.2.108–20), that Prospero has magical books he will drown.

The spectators who first saw Shakespeare's plays — the audience he wrote for—perceived them in much the same way we do now; our brains operate similarly, and on similar materials. What has changed is cultural values, practices, and conditioning. In an earlier study, *Shakespeare's Webs*, I attempted to bring various, even conflicting, early modern cultural meanings to bear on specific stage properties as a way of transhistorically recovering early significations of the plays — ways in which Richard II's mirror or Lear's map were viewed that in time led to interpreting much of the play that contained them. In the present study, I want to attempt the same recovery by considering stage properties essential to a scene's or a play's meaning but that are nevertheless not seen at all, such as the crown that Antony thrice offers to Julius Caesar or the turquoise Leah gave to Shylock when he was a bachelor and that Jessica would trade for a pet monkey. Such properties can lead us not only backward to initial meanings, but forward to seeing many of Shakespeare's plays in new and multiple ways. When we move beyond the idea of a single source for each play and accept instead the various instincts and judgments active in Shakespeare's time – the various neural pathways potential in a single Shakespearean play – we will come much closer to bringing the plays back to the experience they knew at the Curtain, the Fortune, and the Globe.

Newcastle, Brisbane, and Melbourne, Australia
Amherst, Massachusetts
August 2005

ARISTOTLE'S LEGACY

I

None teacheth true philosophy but Aristotle.

— **John Lyly,** *Campaspe* **(4.1.51-52)**

"All men by nature desire to know" (980a1):[1] the foundation of all Aristotle's thought is the opening sentence of his *Metaphysics*. It is the deep need to know and to understand himself and the world around him that is, for Aristotle, not only man's essential characteristic but precisely that which sets him apart from all other terrestrial beings. It is also what in turn makes philosophy—the study of knowing and of knowledge—man's primary intellectual endeavor. Man's unique brain, with all of its elaborate circuitry, was created that he might reason, learn and know. And yet, for Aristotle, knowledge begins not in the brain but with the senses, the most important of which is sight.

> All men by nature desire to know. An indication of this is the delight we take in our senses, for even apart from their usefulness they are loved for themselves—and above all others, the sense of sight. For not only with a view to action, but even when we are not going to do anything, we prefer seeing (one might say) to everything else. The reason is that this, most of all the

> senses, makes us know and brings to light many differences between things (980a26–7).

Earlier, Plato, Aristotle's teacher, had sharply distinguished "higher" and "lower" human senses; vision and hearing were the higher senses, those which exalted man on his intellectual journey toward understanding the natural and supernatural worlds, the world of man and the world of gods, physics, and metaphysics. But Aristotle grounds such understanding in material things – "The object of sight is the visible, and what is visible is (a) colour and (b) a certain kind of object" (*De Anima* II.7 [418a26–27], tr. J.A. Smith in McKeon, p. 567); in contact with such objects or seeing them at a distance, whether merely mechanical or qualitative, the reception and effect of objects by man's vision leads to perception and from that to understanding. Reason, man's peculiar task, is possible only through such perception, as Aristotle makes clear later on in the *Metaphysics* (X.3):

> Things are like if, not being absolutely the same, nor without difference in respect of their concrete substance, they are the same in form; e.g., the larger square is like the smaller, and unequal straight lines are like; they are like, but not absolutely the same. Other things are like, if having the same form, and being things in which difference of degree is possible, they have no difference of degree. Other things, if they have a quality that is in form one and the same—e.g., whiteness—in a greater or lesser degree, are called like because their form is one. Other things are called like if the qualities they have in common are more numerous than those in which they differ—either the qualities in general or the prominent qualities; e.g., tin is like silver, *qua* white, and gold is like fire, *qua* yellow and red (1054b).
>
> States of knowledge are neither innate in a determinate form, nor developed from other higher states of knowledge, but from sense-perception.[2]

We learn to identify and conceptualize by comparison and contrast; our vision is necessary in this building process.

Aristotle returns to a discussion of sight in *De Anima* (II.6–7). Later in his discussion he notes the distinction between what we would call sight of objects and the perception of them:

> … if to perceive by sight is just to see, and what is seen is colour (or the coloured), then if we are to see that which sees, that

> which sees originally must be coloured. It is clear therefore that "to perceive by sight" has more than one meaning; for even when we are not seeing, it is by sight that we discriminate darkness from light, though not in the same way as we distinguish one colour from another. Further, in a sense even that which sees is coloured; for in each case the sense-organ is capable of receiving the sensible object without its matter. That is why even when the sensible objects are gone the sensings and imaginings continue to exist in the sense-organs. (425b17–25)

Knowledge begins with objects—stage properties, speaking theatrically—and we learn to identify, characterize, and interpret by accumulating individual instances, by accumulation and by discernment. A stage crown, as we shall see in the next chapter, can be an imperial crown, or a regal crown, or a coronet, but each kind of crown gets its own definition through an accumulation of examples and a further discrimination among them, a process that depends first of all on seeing the crown (in the eye or conceptually, in the mind's eye) and then relating it to its context as well as to other examples of crowns (or coronets). We enlarge on this when we claim knowledge is the vision of some thing that is processed by the brain along neural pathways and across synapses worn down by frequent usage.

This classical understanding of the need for knowledge and the activity of the mind was later preserved and promulgated by medieval thinkers such as Thomas Aquinas. He too claims in the *Summa Theologica* that "the sight [is] the most perfect, and the most universal of all the senses" (laQ.78, Art.3),[3] (although Thomas would add that spiritual understanding of an object is even more desirable than a material understanding of it); moreover, he would replace object with image. Thus, contending that "The Philosopher," by whom Thomas means Aristotle, "proves that the origin of knowledge is from the senses:"

> I answer that, On this point, the philosophers held three opinions. For Democritus held that all knowledge is caused by images issuing from the bodies we think of and entering into our souls, as Augustine says in his letter to Dioscorus. And Aristotle says that Democritus held that knowledge is caused by a discharge of images. And the reason for this opinion was that both Democritus and the other early philosophers did not distinguish between intellect and sense, as Aristotle relates. Consequently, since the sense is immuted [transformed] by the sensible, they thought that all our knowledge is caused merely

> by an immutation from sensible things. This immutation Democritus held to be caused by a discharge of images. [But] according to Plato, neither does intellectual knowledge proceed from sensible knowledge, nor does sensible knowledge itself come entirely from sensible things; but these rouse the sensible soul to sensation, and the senses likewise rouse the intellect to the act of understanding.
>
> Aristotle chose a middle course (laQ.84, Art. 6).

Thomas is clear enough about Aristotle's singular use of the senses for the cause of later knowledge, but he would tread the middle way between Democritus and Plato as well. He concludes (laQuestion 85, Article 3), by proposing that:

> There are two operations in the sensitive part. One is limited to immutation, and thus the operation of the senses takes place when the senses are impressed by the sensible. The other is formation, inasmuch as the imagination forms for itself an image of an absent thing, or even of something never seen. Both of these operations are found in the intellect. For in the first place there is the passion of the possible intellect as informed by the intelligible species; and then the possible intellect, as thus informed, then forms a definition, or a division, or a composition, which is expressed by language.

In his *Commentary on the Metaphysics of Aristotle*, Thomas expands further on Aristotle's own remarks on sight:

> Our senses serve us in two respects: in knowing things and in meeting the needs of life, we love them for themselves inasmuch as they enable us to know and also assist us to live. This is evident from the fact that all men take the greatest delight in that sense which is most knowing, i.e., the sense of sight, which we value not merely in order to do something, but even when we are not required to act at all.[4]

In his important study of *Theories of Cognition in the Later Middle Ages*, Robert Pasnau writes more broadly of the Scholastics that medieval philosophy drew a sharp line between sense and intellect.

> Where we now see a sequence of processes from eye to inner brain that resists any simple bifurcation into the sensory and

> the intellectual, the medievals saw a clear break. One reason it was natural for them to see such a break is that they took the sensory faculties to operate through physical organs, whereas they took intellectual cognition to be entirely a nonphysical process.

But he concentrates on Thomas, and his sense of cognition growing out of Aristotle:

> Sensory activity regularly takes place without imagination or memory. But Aquinas holds that true intellectual cognition requires forming a mental word. "It belongs to the nature of intellective cognition that in cognizing intellect forms something." Intellectual activity without the formation of a mental word is mere thinking without understanding. Aquinas also seems to think of the internal senses as storehouses for images that can be called up when desired.[5]

Thomas' substitution of image for object allows him to admit the imagination, the idea of composition and the employment of language. Thus, there can be verbal as well as intellectual reference to the initiating object and this referential way of establishing meaning can be expanded to permit objects that are absent or never even seen. Such an expansion is striking: rather than gain knowledge from an actual crown, such as the one Henry IV lays beside him and that Prince Hal picks up, thinking his father dead, a crown we see in the performance of *2 Henry IV*, Thomas would add to our ability to know the absent crown that Antony offers Caesar, which we never see. Both the seen and the unseen work relationally (as different seen crowns would for Aristotle) and both now help us to constitute the possible significations of crown. "Aquinas," sums Pasnau, "shares the presupposition, characteristic of seventeenth-century philosophy, that the immediate and direct objects of cognitive apprehension are our internal impressions" (p. 293).

Such ideas were transmitted to the Renaissance by Leonardo da Vinci whose *Notebooks* add an early scientific understanding to the use of sight as the basis of knowledge that aligns the physical functions of the eye and brain with that of present-day cognitive scientists. According to Leonardo:

> The pupil of the eye which receives through a very small round hole the images of bodies situated beyond this hole always

> receives them upside down and the visual faculty always sees them upright as they are. And this proceeds from the fact that the said images pass through the centre of the crystalline sphere situated in the middle of the eye; and in this centre they unite in a point and then spread themselves out upon the opposite surface of this sphere without deviating from their course; and the images direct themselves upon this surface according to the object that has caused them, and from thence they are taken by the impression and transmitted to the common sense where they are judged (fol. D2v).[6]

Elsewhere in the *Notebooks*, Leonardo records that:

> The intersections of the images at the entrance of the pupil do not mingle one in another in that space where this intersection unites them; and this is evident because if the rays of the sun pass through two panes of glass in contact one with another, the one of these being blue and the other yellow, the ray that penetrates them does not assume the hue of blue or yellow but of a most beautiful green. And the same process would occur with the eye if the images yellow and green in colour should come to mingle one with the other at the intersection which they make within themselves at the entrance of the pupil, but as this does not happen such a mingling does not exist (p. 247).

Leonardo's sophisticated sense of the way in which the sight of objects enters the eye is much the same as scientists hold today, but the mingling of images that can occur before common sense interprets ("judges") them and the understanding of the way in which images are processed by the brain is still elementary in his work. What Leonardo's more primitive attempts at a scientific analysis of sight do, however, is emphasize what Aristotle had introduced, the essential priority of sight for knowledge, for the making of meaning. Leonardo's extensive concern with optics underscores Aristotle's emphasis on sight in the *Metaphysics* and Thomas' additional observations on the importance of images in the *Summa*.

II

I wold begin with the eye, as a light to all the rest.

— **John Lyly,** *Campaspe* **(3.4.84)**

"Vision is the dominant human sense," Nicholas Humphrey writes. "It is the sense that has been most widely studied by psychologists and mulled over by philosophers; and it is the sense for which the distinction between the intimate role of sensation and the defining role of perception is most difficult to draw."[7] This was especially true in amorphic paintings executed on two different but intersecting visual planes. One example is the portrait of young Edward VI in the privy gallery at Whitehall palace overlooking the tiltyard—a place where Shakespeare's company played. At first, "'the head, face and nose appear so long and misformed that they do not seem to represent a human being,'" but if a viewer extended an iron bar with a plate attached to it and looked through a hole in the plate, "'the ugly face changed into a well-formed one.'"[8] Popular curio cabinets also concentrated on visual objects. Thomas Platter records seeing a wonder-cabinet of the merchant-adventurer Thomas Cope, stuffed with an African charm made out of teeth, a bauble and bell once owned by the fool of Henry VIII, an Indian axe and canoe, a chain made of monkey teeth, a Madonna made out of an Indian feather, a unicorn's tail, and a worldwide collection of shoes.[9]

Indeed, the theater as a place for watching was always a concern of the Master of Revels, Edmund Tillney, who, James Shapiro tells us, could "scrutinize a dress performance [of plays performed at Christmas] at the Revels office to ensure that nothing *visual* or verbal would give offense" (p.31; my emphasis). He knew sight was primary. As Frederick Kiefer observes in *Shakespeare's Visual Theatre*,

> When Elizabethan and Jacobean playgoers approached a public theatre, they would first have encountered a painted sign identifying the structure, and when they walked inside, they discovered a combination of textiles and painted wood intended to provide visual delight. Although the sole surviving depiction of a theatrical interior (in an outdoor playhouse) contemporaneous with Shakespeare shows a building with little adornment, the artist's accompanying comments indicate that the decoration was splendid. The covering over the stage of the Swan theatre, Johannes De Witt reports, was "supported by

> wooden columns painted in such excellent imitation of marble that it is able to deceive even the most cunning." Another record (of a trickster who promised an entertainment at the Swan and then absconded with the money) tells us about some of the interior furnishings: "the common people, when they saw themselves deluded, revenged themselves upon the hangings, curtains, chairs, stooles, walles, and whatsoever came in their way." ... Playgoers saw other sorts of decoration too. The contract for the Fortune theatre calls for carved satyrs to be set atop posts of the structure's frame and stage. The drawings by Inigo Jones of the Cockpit in Drury Lane depict statues within niches on either side of the main opening onto the stage; the arch above the doorway is supported by two Doric columns; and draped above the two subsidiary doors are festoons of foliage. The underside of the superstructure covering the Globe stage was painted to simulate the sky, probably the stars, possibly even the signs of the zodiac. The rebuilt Globe theatre in London, with its carved figures over the stage, brilliantly painted tiring-house, and decorated ceiling above the playing area, today provides some idea of the splendor that must have confronted Shakespeare's playgoers.[10]

Kiefer continues by noting that, "On the stage even the most ordinary things may possess symbolic import. Consider the hand props that figure in dramatic action: goblets, swords, lutes, letters, candles, handkerchiefs, purses, keys, flowers, and other everyday items" (p. 11) and cites Richard of Gloucester's appearance between two bishops, a prayerbook in his hand (*Richard III*, 3.7.95 s.d.); Richard II shattering the mirror Bullingbrook hands him (4.1.288s.d.); and Kent in the stocks, reproducing on the stage common sixteenth-century prints that showed evil putting virtue in the stocks (*King Lear*, 2.4.1 s.d; Kiefer, pp. 11–12).

Thus, the drama of Shakespeare and his contemporaries stressed the visual.[11] There is the prologue to *Tamburlaine I*, for instance—

> From jigging veins of rhyming mother-wits
> And such conceits as clownage keeps in pay,
> We'll lead you to the stately tent of war,
> Where you shall hear the Scythian Tamburlaine
> Threatening the world with high astounding terms,
> And scourging kingdoms with his conquering sword.
> View but his picture in this tragic glass,

And then applaud his fortunes as you please. (1–8) [12]

David Riggs notes further that nearly all the contemporary allusions and actions in *Tamburlaine I* center on three sights or "notorious images: the caged Bajazeth; the display of white, red and black colours on successive days to convey Tamburlaine's orders for the citizens to evacuate a besieged town; and the team of captive kings drawing Tamburlaine's chariot."[13] In a letter of September 1610, Henry Jackson reports on a production of *Othello* he saw at Oxford where he was most moved by what he saw: "But that Desdemona, murdered by her husband in our presence, although she always pled her case excellently, yet when killed moved us more, while stretched out on her bed she begged the spectators' pity with her very facial expressions."[14] Indeed, Ruth Lunney finds plays were "particularly rich in … visual signs that directed attention to conventional understandings, and exploited conventional ironies: the mutilation of Lavinia in *Titus Andronicus*, for example, or the deformity of Richard III, or the penitential robes of the Duchess of Gloucester (*2 Henry VI*). More generally, in play after play, there were crowns and swords, beds and thrones, daggers and halters, kneelings and embracings, processions of triumph and the bodies of the once-powerful littering the stage."[15] Hamlet insists on seeing the Ghost; Othello insists on ocular proof of Desdemona's infidelity. *In A Warning for Fair Women* (1599), Tragedy, Comedy, and History compete for superiority until History remarks, "Look, Comedy, I mark'd it not till now, The stage is hung with blacke, and I perceive The auditor's prepar'd for tragedie."[16] Properties were among the most valuable possessions of an acting company; as early as 1567, those collected at the Bell Inn were hired out for additional income; as late as 1593, when players returned to a plague-ravaged London from a tour that was largely unsuccessful, the last thing they did to recover their losses was to sell their properties.

The illustrated title-pages of plays reinforce their visual significance and power. The woodcut for the 1615 edition of Thomas Kyd's *Spanish Tragedy* shows Horatio hanging in the garden, his riding boots still on. To the right stands his father Hieronimo who, with the aid of a lighted torch, has just discovered him. His wife Isabella stands to the right. The signs of brutality shown on both sides of Hieronimo demonstrate how the words that stream from his mouth go unheeded, his sorrow unrecognized and unacknowledged by others. The 1630 quarto of Robert Greene's play about Friar Bacon and Friar Bungay shows Bacon's brazen head on top of the shelf of

The Spanish Tragedie:

OR,

Hieronimo is mad againe.

Containing the lamentable end of *Don Horatio*, and *Belimperia*; with the pittifull death of *Hieronimo*.

Newly corrected, amended, and enlarged with new Additions of the *Painters* part, and others, as it hath of late been diuers times acted.

LONDON,
Printed by W. White, for I. White and T. Langley,
and are to be ſold at their Shop ouer againſt the
Sarazens head without New-gate. 1615.

Figure 1: Title page of Thomas Kyd's *The Spanish Tragedy* (1615)

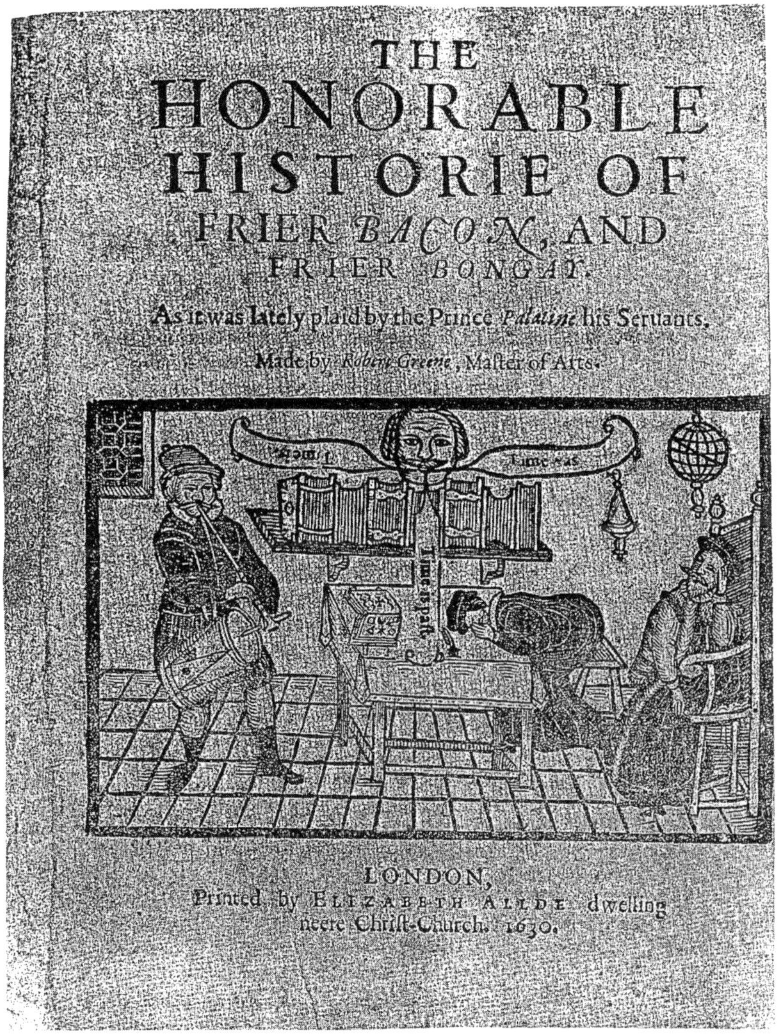
THE
HONORABLE
HISTORIE OF
FRIER BACON, AND
FRIER BONGAY.
As it was lately plaid by the Prince *Palatine* his Seruants.
Made by *Robert Greene*, Maſter of Arts.

LONDON,
Printed by ELIZABETH ALLDE dwelling
neere Chriſt-Church. 1630.

Figure 2: Title page of Robert Greene's *Friar Bacon and Friar Bungay* (1630)

The Tragicall Hiſtory of the Life and Death of Doctor FAVSTVS.

With new Additions.

Written by *Ch. Mar.*

Printed at London for *Iohn Wright*, and are to be ſold at his ſhop without Newgate, 1624.

Figure 3: Title page of Christopher Marlowe's *Dr. Faustus* (1631)

Figure 4: Title page of the anonymous *Arden of Faversham* (1633)

scholarly books pronouncing its mystical truths—"Time is," "Time is past," "Time was"—to the beat of Time's drum while the two friars, asleep, fail to hear the oracular words. While the shelf of books denotes Bacon's scholarship, the book that lies open on the table is a book of magical sayings; the celestial orb at the top right of the woodcut reminds us of Roger Bacon's interest in the heavens. The illustration of Christopher Marlowe's *Doctor Faustus*, printed in 1631, portrays Faustus as, simultaneously, a scholar with a book in his study; a magician with a magic robe; and a humanist wearing his humanist's hat. Magical signs hang on the wall to our left and on the shelf to the right, while below the shelf a cross represents Christianity, holding down Mephastophilis in the shape of the devil. The 1633 quarto of the anonymous *Arden of Faversham* shows the murder of Thomas Arden by Shakebag and Black Will during a game of backgammon in Arden's parlor, while Mosby, the lover of Arden's wife, enters from the garden and Arden's wife Alice, on the left, and Susan, Mosby's sister and Alice Arden's serving-maid, extend their knives toward the victim.

Shakespeare pays considerable attention to sight throughout his works. An early play such as *Love's Labor's Lost* is indicative. "Your light grows dark by losing of your eyes," Berowne tells the King of Navarre in the play's opening scene, and adds:

> Study me how to please the eye indeed
> By fixing it upon a fairer eye,
> Who dazzling so, that eye shall be his heed,
> And give him light that it was blinded by (1.1. 80–83).

Boyet later tells the Princess "Methought all [the King's] senses were lock'd in his eye" (2.1. 242) and Berowne in time agrees—at considerable length (4.3. 324–30)

But the stage also offered recollections that motivated the mind's eye. In Marlowe's play of *Dido, Queen of Carthage* (1594), we learn of the Greek massacre of the Trojans only by report:

> Young infants swimming in their parents' blood,
> Headless carcasses piled up in heaps,
> Virgins half-dead, dragged by their golden hair
> And with main force flung on a ring of pikes,
> Old men with swords thrust through their aged sides,
> Kneeling for mercy to a Greekish lad,
> Who with steel pole-axes dashed out their brains.[17]

In *Cymbeline*, Jachimo takes down an inventory of Imogen's bedroom on his tablet, "Such and such pictures; there the window; such Th' adornment of her bed; the arras, figures" (2.2.25–26), so that he can recreate the room in all its detail when he returns to Posthumus (2.4). In the masque at Timon's banquet, Cupid remarks:

Hail to thee, worthy Timon , and to all
That of his bounties taste! The five best senses
Acknowledge thee their patron, and come freely
To gratulate thy plenteous bosom. Th'ear,
Taste, touch, smell, all pleased from thy table rise;
They only now come but to feast thine eyes. (1.2.122–27)

Primary emphasis is awarded sight. The entire play of *Much Ado about Nothing* revolves around the scene at Hero's window that no playgoer ever sees, the source of the much ado. We know that Claudio — who does see it — is tricked because Borachio tells Conrad about the trick of substituting Margaret (3.3.144–63) before Claudio misunderstands, misinterprets, and dismisses Hero at the moment in the wedding when he is to pledge his love. He has trusted his ears rather than his eyes, Don John's false report rather than his more accurate vision (3.2.88–134). The friar who was to perform the marriage knows better, because he has seen Hero directly and judges her accurately.

Hear me a little,
For I have only been silent so long,
And given way unto this course of fortune,
By noting of the lady I have mark'd
A thousand blushing apparitions
To start into her face, a thousand innocent shames
In angel whiteness beat away those blushes,
And in her eye there hath appear'd a fire
To burn the errors that these princes held
Against her maiden truth. Call me a fool,
Trust not my reading, nor my observations,
Which with experimental seal doth warrant
The tenor of my book; trust not my age,
My reverence, calling, nor divinity,
If this sweet lady lie not guiltless here
Under some biting error (4.1.155–70)

The Friar—like Aristotle, like Shakespeare—knows the primacy of sight, knows its greater reliability: "I have marked"; "my observations." But Shakespeare also knew that when sights—viewing objects, seeing events—occur offstage, playgoers are stimulated to use their mind's eye, their substitute way of seeing as a substitute way of knowing. This is what gives his plays indeterminacy at key moments. This is what keeps his playing alive, performance after performance—the stimulation of cognition by imagined sight.

III

> I fear me, Apelles, that thine eyes have blabbed that which thy tongue durst not.
>
> — **John Lyly,** *Campaspe* **(5.2.1–2)**

"We do not see what we sense," Tør Norretranders acknowledges; "We see what we think we sense."[18] The matter of seeing is really a matter of thinking. "When we talk of 'seeing,' " write Paul M. Matthews and Jeffrey McQuain, "we are not speaking of eyes at all; we are speaking of an activity of the brain. The brain activity in 'seeing' occurs specifically in the primary visual cortex, which is found in a thin rim of gray matter at the back of the brain along the inner surface of each hemisphere. As in other areas of the brain, the neurons in the visual cortex and their organization are highly specialized."[19] The human retina contains roughly 126 million rods and cones, photoreceptors that sense the wavelength and intensity of light and convert this data into neural impulses, a language that the brain can understand. The retina does not process all of the light it receives; that would be overpowering. Rather, it selects the data it wishes to process, allowing less than ten percent to pass through to the brain. Such selectivity helps us to see better and the brain to process more comprehensively. Still, our initial vision has certain limitations. We see, first of all, only what is in front of our eyes; we do not experience vividly objects or actions that are peripheral. We see surfaces, not depths. We see in two, not three, dimensions. And we see from a certain perspective—both from a certain distance and from a certain angle.[20]

Normal vision of an object provides the retina with an image of approximately 120 million rods along with about 6 million cones that are responsible for splitting into specialized information such as motion, color, and form. Fragmented portions of images, movements, and wavelengths are sent to the various visual centers in the brain

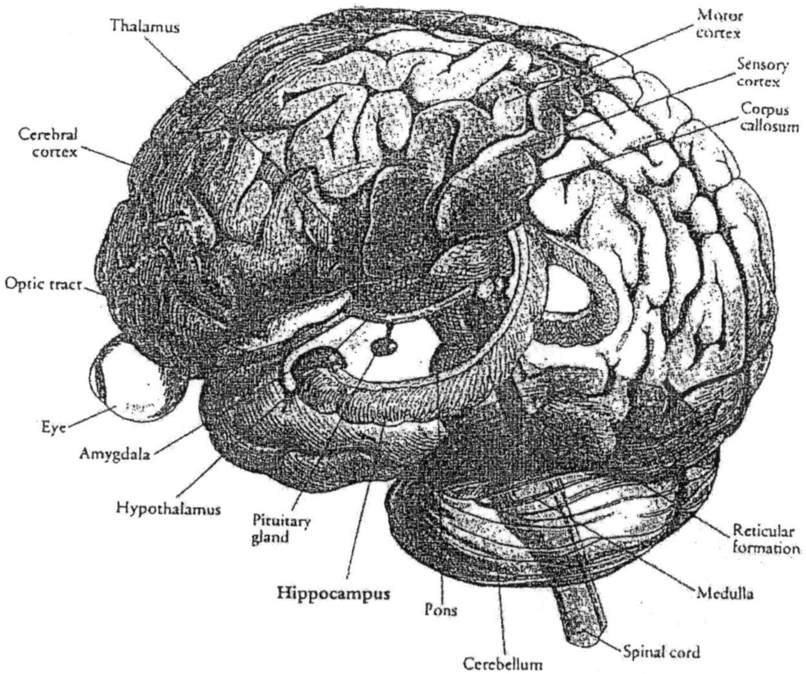

Figure 5: The brain, reprinted from V.S. Ramachandran and Sandra Blakeslee, *Phantoms in the Brain*

where a visual memory stores image patterns. If there is a match, the object is instantly recognized. The brain's function is to restore gaps when incomplete data can result in misperceptions or visual illusions. A chemical in the eye, rhodopsin, is what changes light energy into neural energy and information to allow for such rapid transit: information reaches the brain's visual areas from the retina in approximately fifty milliseconds.

Neuroscientists can now trace this process in considerably more detail. Visual messages pass from the eye by way of the optic nerve to the lateral geniculate nucleus in the thalamus before proceeding to the cerebral cortex of the brain. Axons from the lateral geniculate nucleus project to the occipital lobes of the cerebral cortex, where the visual signal is processed in the area known as V (for visual) 1. From V1, neural information passes on to V2, where the neurons are separated and sent to V3, which handles form; V4, which deals with color; or V5, which is concerned with movement; and as many as 25 other visual areas that handle specific aspects of the visual image. All these areas, however, take part in two major pathways of visual information, that known as the "where" pathway that progresses from the occipital lobe dorsally into the parietal lobe and locates an object and orients the subject toward it; and that known as the "what" pathway, moving from the occipital lobe ventrally into the temporal lobe to identify objects.[21] "The brain is the most complex object in the universe," John J. Ratney sums, continuing:

> There are a hundred billion neurons in a single human brain, and roughly ten times as many other cells that have noncomputational roles. Each of these neurons is connected to others by branching treelike projections known as axons and dendrites, most of which terminate in tiny structures called synapses. Synapses are the subject of much current brain research, for it is believed that most learning and development occurs in the brain through the process of strengthening or weakening these connections. Each one of our hundred billion neurons may have anywhere from 1 to 10,000 synaptic connections to other neurons. This means that the theoretical number of different patterns of connections possible in a single brain is approximately 40,000,000,000,000,000—forty quadrillion. It is in the tiny synaptic gaps, where an electrical signal is briefly transformed into a chemical one and back again, [that] different electrochemical configurations in a single brain come to a staggering number: ten to the trillionth power (pp. 9–11).

The brain is thus largely composed of associational networks: a web of neural cross-firings that make certain synapses strong from frequent use; and because this varies from individual to individual, the visual patterns and perceptions that emerge from the brain can vary enormously. "The exact web of connections among neurons at a particular moment," says Ratney, "is determined [also] by a combination of genetic makeup, environment, the sum of experiences we've imposed on our brains, and the activity we are bombarding it with now and each second into the future. What we do moment to moment greatly influences how the web continually reweaves itself" (p. 26). Our biographies, our cultural pressures, and our personal values all contribute to the information that the brain processes, that contribute to the associative patterns that help to determine what it is we see.

Harold Love has refined this understanding further:

> Even in the brains of identical twins, formed when the zygote divides after conception, tiny irregularities in the laying down

> of neural pathways become magnified into differences in the ways by which the brain, as a self-organising system, coordinates its vast assemblage of centres and individual neurons in the acts of knowing, speaking and writing. Experience stocks all brains with different knowledge, perceptions and attitudes. On the other hand, since language is also a shared possession with communal as well as self-expressive functions, what nature and experience individualise will often be overwritten by socialisation.[22]

Shakespeare's age had a simplified sense of such a process. In his *Defence of Ryme* (1603), Samuel Daniel speaks of "excellent conceits, whose scattered limbs we are fain to look out and join together."[23] In another sense, Erasmus' *De Duplici Copia Verborum ac Rerum* (the *De Copia*, first published in England in 1569), teaches that commonplaces (*loci communes*) need to be arranged from separate sayings into patterns; in placing sayings into pigeonholes ready to extract when needed, this is in a simplified way what is going on with far more complexity as the neural pathways in the brain make their associational connections. Without frequent and constant use, though, precepts and concepts in the brain fade, are continually modified by new and related precepts, or can in time disappear altogether. Stored visual precepts form the memory, but the traces of memory, growing ever more dim unless exercised, can distort new data by contaminating it. This is what allows for faulty or distorted patterns. Data stored in the brain, moreover, can be activated to seal shortcomings or lapses in a visual patterning. The process is analogous to the blind spot that we all have in our vision, a blind spot first predicted by the seventeenth-century French scientist Edme Mariotte. "While dissecting a human eye," V.S. Ramachandran and Sandra Blakeslee report, "Mariotte noticed the optic disk—the area of the retina where the optic nerve exits the eyeball. He realized that unlike other parts of the retina, the optic disk is not sensitive to light. Applying his knowledge of optics and eye anatomy, he deduced that every eye should be blind in a small portion of its visual field."[24] And so it is. But the brain does not simply ignore the blind spot, seeing it as a hole in the visual field it is processing. Rather, it fills out the visual image by supplying properties that will complete such an image. This is, in a way, the most frequent employment of the "mind's eye."

To recapitulate: visual stimuli enter the brain in an undifferentiated stream of electrical impulses created by neurons firing along a certain pathway, often one well worn through previous activity. The brain divides the incoming impulses into different streams toward different modules in the cerebral cortex—what Rita Carter calls "the wrinkled outer grey skin where sights and sounds are put together and then made conscious."[25] At the same time, other stimuli enter the limbic system, where emotional reactions are generated. Once the differentiated stimuli are processed and reassembled, once "sensory perceptions are married with appropriate cognitive associations," as Carter puts it (p. 108), the new configurations are returned to meaningful perception. But "by the time we think we know something—[by the time] it is part of our conscious experience—the brain has already done its work," Michael S. Gazzaniga concludes.

> Systems built into the brain do their work automatically and largely outside of our conscious awareness. The brain finishes the work half a second before the information it processes reaches our consciousness. That most of the brain is engaged in activities outside conscious awareness should come as no surprise. This great zone of cerebral activity is where plans are made to speak, write, throw a baseball, or pick up a dish from the table. We are clueless about how all this works and gets effected. We don't plan or articulate these activities. We simply observe the output. This fact of brain–mind organization is as true for simple perceptual acts as it is for higher-order activities like spatial behavior, mathematics, and even language. The brain begins to cover for this "done deal" aspect of its functioning by creating in us the illusion that the events we are experiencing are happening in real time—not before our conscious experience of deciding to do something.[26]

Our reactions to stage spectacles are identical. We think we interpret consciously what we see much as anyone else would, when in fact we are experiencing the consequences, not the activities, of our brain's interpretation of selective data that reflects our own particular configurations of neurons and neural pathways. None of us sees a stage spectacle—or a stage property—identically, although nearly all of us perceive that spectacle or property in broadly agreeable, constituent, form. "We do not see what we sense. We see what we think we sense."

IV

> The eyes are two open windows to the soul. Nothing entereth more effectually into memory than that which cometh of seeing. Things heard pass lightly away, but the tokens of that which we have seen stick fast in us, whether we will or no.
>
> **Anthony Munday,** *Blast of Retrait from Playes and Theatres*

Vision gives rise, therefore, to the brain's perception and thought, but linked as it is with memory and experience, it is always individual. Aristotle makes such a connection in the *Posterior Analytics*: "Out of sense-perception comes to be what we call memory, and out of frequently repeated memories of the same thing develops experience; for a number of memories constitute a single experience" (100a).[27] But in his *De Memoria*, Aristotle is equally clear that vision begins with images of objects—either those seen, such as the rings Portia and Nerissa exchange with Bassanio and Gratiano, or those that are absent, such as Leah's turquoise that Jessica abandons for a monkey. Aristotle notes that:

> We cannot think without imagery, for the same phenomenon occurs in thinking as is found in the construction of geometrical figures; there, though we do not employ as a supplementary requirement of our proof a determinateness in the size of the triangle, yet when we draw it we make a determinate size. Similarly in thinking also, though we do not think of the size, yet we present the object visually to ourselves as a quantum, though we do not think of it as a quantum. If the nature of the object be quantitative but indeterminate, our presentation is of a determinate quantity, though we think of it as quantitative merely.
>
> The reason why we think of nothing apart from continuity and cannot think of objects not in time apart from time, belongs to a different inquiry from this, but we must apprehend magnitude and change by the same means as that by which we are conscious of time. Imagery is a phenomenon belonging to the common sense; so this is clear, that the apprehension of those determinations belongs to the primary organ of sensation: and memory, even the memory of concepts, cannot exit apart from imagery (450a7–13).[28]

Imagery is an object visually seen, like the ring, when it is neurally processed to and by the brain; it is what the brain sends to conscious thought and stores in the memory. For Aristotle, all images are cognitive, as today's neuroscience employs images derived from sense-impressions.

We have just seen how the brain processes sense-impressions, but neuroscientists have also advanced our understanding of just how memory operates. In his recent study, Ratney summarizes their findings:

> A memory is only made when it is called upon. In its quiescent state it is not detectable. Therefore we cannot separate the act of retrieving and the memory itself. Indeed, bits and pieces of a single memory are stored in different networks of neurons all around the brain. We bring the pieces together when it is time to recall that memory. We pull the pants, shirt, and shoes out of different parts of the closet to re-create the single image of how we looked last Monday, when we thought we looked so good. When the day is over we put the pieces back, and even if they're not in exactly the same places we still know where to find them and how to put them together again. … Memories—from two minutes, two years, and two decades ago—come and go every waking hour. Each one arises from a vast network of interconnected pieces. The pieces are units of language, emotions, beliefs, and actions, and here, right away, comes the first surprising conclusion: because our daily experiences constantly alter these connections, a memory is a tiny bit different each time we remember it (p. 186).

But time is not all that can influence memory. Frequency of recall has its fundamental effect: just as neural pathways and synapses are strengthened through use and weakened through disuse, so a person's mood, or his surroundings, or his initial memory pattern may differ, even from those around him. No one is "right" or "wrong"; he can merely differ in his perceptions and therefore in his recollections. As new related memories are added, the original memory of the original event can also be modified or even, in time, displaced by later memories of related images. Conversely, memories can become so powerful that they seem to get stuck like a phonograph record: Lady Macbeth's persistent washing of her hands is an instance where a single moment is memorialized at the expense of all that preceded it and all that came after.

Moreover, memories can be affected not just by the brain's cortex but by the amygdala. As Ratney explains it:

> The frontal cortex is the part of the brain that neatly organizes the bits and pieces into a temporal, logical, and "meaningful" story. However, it must be set in motion by the amygdala, which proves an emotional tag to a memory, a "meaning" that helps cement the pieces. Given this, one's emotional state at a given instant affects how the amygdala processes the emotional tag of a memory, perhaps changing ever so slightly how that memory is reconstructed. An individual who is depressed is predisposed to see a certain memory in a negative light—so it's a different kind of memory than it would have been had the person been generally happy (p. 186).

Ratney gives an example of a woman who is delighted when her boss helps her to write a memo; because the company is laying off workers, she takes this as a sign that her job is not endangered. But as dismissals increase, she creates a quite different story, deciding that her boss helped her because she was inadequate at her job and is therefore threatened herself with dismissal (pp. 186–87). "The string of events in the memory may be the same," Ratney concludes, "but the tone and hence the meaning are very different" (p. 187).

Neuroscience has not yet determined where constituent images of the memory may be kept, although in *Descartes's Error*, Antonio Damasio has proposed "convergence zones" near the sensory neurons that first register the images. "Mounting evidence," though, "suggests that the hippocampus might serve as the master regulator, the hub at the center of the wheel," Ratney writes. "The hippocampus does not store memories. It has been likened to an intelligent collating machine, which filters new associations, decides what is important and what to ignore or compress, sorts the results, and then sends various packets of information to other parts of the brain. It is a way station that hands out the pieces" (p. 188).

As a playwright, Shakespeare is as concerned with the pieces as with the configurations of them and the fact that such configurations may change over time. The will that Portia's father leaves her in *The Merchant of Venice* is one that stipulates a contest involving the choice of the right casket to win Portia as a wife; and Portia finds the will blocks her desires, then is a burden she must continually carry, and finally becomes a document she can make to serve her own ends in choosing Bassanio as she directs his choice among gold, silver, and lead. The absent property—the father's will—thus has several inherent meanings, while other wills in other Shakespearean plays take on still other configurations. Some of these meanings are situational, to be sure; but others are culturally determined, and still others result from personal circumstances and perspectives. However intuitively sophisticated Shakespeare may or may not have been in understanding how the human brain functions—how men and women perceive and conceive—his plays often rely securely on stage properties both seen and unseen. John C. Meagher has recalled "A very old churchly proverb [that] alleges that to sing a prayer is the equivalent of saying it twice," and he adds by analogy, "an implicitly Shakespearean dramaturgical proverb might claim that to ground and manifest a meaning in a prop is to stage it twice."[29] Knowing how the brains of Shakespeare's playgoers functioned, in the chapters ahead we will look at his stage properties that are offstage to determine how they might have functioned—and have given cognitive significance—that can help to recapture how the plays were received in his own time and how variously they might have then been interpreted.

SHAKESPEARE'S CROWNS

Amidst the celebration of the Feast of Lupercal that opens *The Tragedy of Julius Caesar*, an apprehensive, overwrought Brutus interrupts the festivities with a jarring premonition. "What means this shouting?" he asks Cassius; "I do fear the people choose Caesar for their king." To the wily Cassius, Brutus is transparent, but he too seizes the moment with a jarring observation as a response that will test Brutus. "Ay, do you fear it?" he says, answering a question with a question, and adds, "Then I must think you would not have it so." Brutus' reply is predictably revealing: "I would not, Cassius, yet I love him," combining a private admission with public conventionality (1.2.79–82). But his anxiety is as constant as the Northern Star. Once the naked runner Antony, Caesar, and his train pass by on their return, Brutus pulls Casca out from among them.

Casca: You pull'd me by the cloak, would you speak with me?
Brutus: Ay, Casca, tell us what hath chanc'd to-day
That Caesar looks so sad.
Casca: Why, you were with him, were you not?
Brutus: I should not then ask Casca what had chanc'd (1.2.216-20).

Cassius' whispered conversation has done nothing to relieve Brutus' fixation. He must have his fears confirmed. So Casca obliges him, at first matter of factly.

Casca: Why, there was a crown offer'd him; and being offer'd him, he put it by with the back of his hand thus, and then the people fell a-shouting.

But this is not enough for the preoccupied Brutus.

Brutus: What was the second noise for?
Casca: Why, for that too.
Brutus: They shouted thrice; what was the last cry for?
Casca: Why, for that too.
Brutus: Was the crown offer'd him thrice?
Casca: Ay, marry, was't, and he put it by thrice, every time gentler than other; and at every putting-by mine honest neighbors shouted (1.2.221–31).

When interrogated, the dispassionate Casca provides a revealing detail — Caesar's progressive denial of the crown grows "gentler"; he is less quick to let it go — but in the narrow focus of Brutus' compulsion to confirm his worst suspicions, he strangely overlooks such a detail. Sensing Brutus' urgency and manipulating it, Cassius tries to extend Casca's report: "Who offer'd him the crown?" For the alert and objective Casca, the whole interchange was incidental and performative, but Brutus is insistently demanding.

Brutus: Tell us the manner of it, gentle Casca.
Casca: I can as well be hang'd as tell the manner of it: it was mere foolery, I did not mark it. I saw Mark Antony offer him a crown — yet 'twas not a crown neither, 'twas one of these coronets — and as I told you, he put it by once, but for all that, to my thinking, he would fain have had it. Then he offer'd it to him again, then he put it by again; but, to my thinking, he was very loath to lay his fingers off it. And then he offer'd it the third time; he put it the third time by; and still as he refus'd it, the rabblement howted, and clapp'd their chopp'd hands, and threw up their sweaty night-caps, and utter'd such a deal of stinking breath, because Caesar refus'd the crown, that it had, almost, chok'd Caesar, for he swounded, and fell down at it; and for mine own part, I durst not laugh, for fear of opening my lips and receiving the bad air (1.2.234-50).

But Casca's deeper sense of what has gone on is lost on both his listeners. Brutus has earlier told Cassius that "I am not gamesome; I do lack some part Of that quick spirit that is in Antony" (1.2.28–29) and Caesar has pointed to the same shortcoming in Cassius:

> I do not know the man I should avoid
> So soon as that spare Cassius. He reads much,
> He is a great observer, and he looks
> Quite through the deeds of men. He loves no plays,
> As thou dost, Antony; he hears no music (1.2.200–04).

Instead, he would turn what Casca senses is theater into a metaphor that drives forward his own plan to ensnare the support of Brutus.

Cassius: But soft I pray you; what, did Caesar swound?
Casca: He fell down in the market-place, and foam'd at mouth, and was speechless.
Brutus: 'Tis very like, he hath the falling sickness.
Cassius: No, Caesar hath it not; but you and I,
And honest Casca, we have the falling sickness (1.2.251–56).

"Tell me, good Brutus," Casca had remarked before Casca arrived, "can you see your face?"

Brutus: No, Cassius; for the eye sees not itself
But by reflection, by some other things.
Cassius: 'Tis just,
And it is very much lamented, Brutus,
That you have no such mirrors as will turn
Your hidden worthiness into your eye,
That you might see your shadow [likeness] ….
Therefore, good Brutus, be prepar'd to hear;
And since you know you cannot see yourself
So well as by reflection, I, your glass,
Will modestly discover to yourself
That of yourself which you yet know not of (1.2.51-70).

This would seem the perfect, irresistible invitation to someone as self-absorbed as Brutus; Marjorie Garber has recently pointed to "Brutus's insistent, almost obsessive use of the word 'I'"[1] in his conversation with Cassius:

That you do love me, I am nothing jealous;
What you would work me to, I have some aim.
How I have thought of this, and of these times,
I shall recount hereafter. For this present,
I would not (so with love I might entreat you)
Be any further mov'd. What you have said
I will consider; what you have to say
I will with patience hear (1.2.162–69).

Left alone, Brutus is the first in the play to pronounce assassination as the aim of the conspirators: "It must be by his death; and for my part, I know no personal cause to spurn at him, But for the general. He would be crown'd" (2.1.10–12). As yet, this is only a presupposition on the part of Brutus; but he has made his cognitive habitus a fact about Caesar and the proper (and permissible) motive for himself. Such an obsession, privately expressed, leads him into peculiar illogicalities:

He would be crown'd:
How that might change his nature, there's the question.
It is the bright day that brings forth the adder,
And that craves wary walking. Crown him that,
And then I grant we put a sting in him
That at his will he may do danger with. …
But 'tis a common proof
That lowliness is young ambition's ladder,
Whereto the climber-upward turns his face;
But when he once attains the upmost round,
He then unto the ladder turns his back,
Looks in the clouds, scorning the base degrees
By which he did ascend. So Caesar may;
Then lest he may, prevent. And since the quarrel
Will bear no color for the thing he is,
Fashion it thus: that what he is, augmented,
Would run to these and these extremities;
And therefore think him as a serpent's egg,
Which hatch'd, would as his kind grow mischievous,
And kill him in the shell (2.1.12–34).

The crown that so haunts Brutus' every thought is here both a motivation and a marker, signified and signifying. The ladder of ambition — the progressive climb to power — has nothing in common with full-blown evil burst from the egg of a serpent, nor would something hatched be susceptible to killing in its shell. Brutus is seizing on commonplaces whether they are consistent or not to further illustrate (and demonstrate) the truth of his own hypothesis. Such a soliloquy is influenced by Cassius, however, for he is now doing exactly what Cassius had told him to do: he is finding himself in the mirror of someone else. The difficulty here is that Brutus wills to mirror himself not in Cassius but in Caesar, or, more precisely, Brutus' version of Caesar. (Such a mirroring will be reversed when Decius Brutus uses the crown to entice Caesar to attend the Senate despite Calpurnia's misgivings and Caesar's own initial refusal at 2.2.94.) Like Caesar, Brutus would have nothing to do with Cicero as an ally — "O, name him not" (2.1.150) — for Cicero penetrates the weakness of them both: "Indeed," Cicero tells Casca:

> it is a strange-disposed time;
> But men may construe things after their fashion,
> Clean from the purpose of the things themselves (1.3.33–35).

Aware of this we, like Shakespeare's first playgoers, are made crucially aware that the necessary scene of revelation — when Antony offered Caesar the crown — is beyond our sight and beyond our certain knowing. We know what Brutus makes of Caesar, but what are we to make of Brutus? And what are we to make of that crown? Or was it, as Casca reports, not a crown at all but a coronet? Differing opinions and judgments of Caesar are registered once more on the same steps of the Forum with the two funeral orations for Caesar by Brutus and Antony (3.2); their cognitive differences register the complexity and uncertainty of how to interpret Caesar that was as crucial to Shakespeare's England as it was to Rome when the English Parliament, like the Roman Senate in the play, was clamoring for more authority under Elizabeth I and James I, whose rule was symbolized in the crowns they wore. Shakespeare's understanding of Caesar, as that of many of his playgoers, was taken directly from Plutarch's *Lives of the Noble Grecians and Romaines* translated by Sir Thomas North out of Amiot's French translation of the Greek original. "After fighting Pompey." Plutarch records, "Caesar being then created Dictator by the Senate, [he] called home againe all the banished men, and restored their children to honour, whose fathers before had bene slaine in Syllaes time: and did somewhat cut off the vsuries that did oppresse them; and besides, did make some such other ordinances as those, but very few. For he was Dictator but eleuen dayes onely, and then did yeeld it vp of himselfe, and made himselfe Counsull" (sigs. 3Q4v-3Q5).[2] Subsequently, "he made three triumphs, ye one for AEGYPT, the other for the kingdome of PONT, and the third for AFRICKE not because he had ouercome Scipio there, but king Iuba" (sig. 3R2v). For Plutarch, Caesar knows how to put such public victories to his own personal advantage; "After these three triumphs ended, he very liberally rewarded his soldiers: & to curry fauour with the people, he made great feasts & cōmon sports. For he feasted all the ROMAINES at one time, at two and twenty thousand tables, & gaue them the pleasure to see diuers sword-players to fight at the sharpe, and battels also by sea, for the remēbrance of his daughter IVLIA, which was dead long before" (sig. 2R2v).

But Plutarch also hints at the triumphant Caesar's imperfections. "Concerning the constitution of his body," Plutarch continues, "he was leane, white, and soft skinned, and often subiect to head-ach, and otherwhile to the falling sicknesse (the which tooke him the first time, as it is reported, in CORDVBA, a city of SPAINE" (sig. 3P6). The three triumphs, then, like the defeat of Pompey, are, for Plutarch, ambivalent matters. As Caesar's power mounts, Plutarch becomes as concerned as Shakespeare's Brutus. "As Cicero the Orator, when one said, tomorrow the starre Lyra will rise; Yes, said he, at the commandement of Caesar, as if men were compelled so to say & thinke, by Caesars edict. But the chiefest cause that made him mortally hated, was the couetous desire he had to be called kinge which first gaue the people iust cause, and next his secret enemies, honest colour to beare him ill will" (sig. 3R3v). Plutarch's mixed evaluation of Caesar — charismatic hero; ambitious tyrant — reaches a crisis, as it does for Shakespeare, at the moment Caesar is offered a crown, the scene Shakespeare deliberately keeps off the stage and out of sight. "So when [Antony] came into the market place," Plutarch writes, "the people made a lane for him to runne at liberty, and he came to Caesar, and presented him a Diademe wreathed about with laurell," the symbol of victory on the battlefield covering a symbol of kingship. That such an offering is theatrical is clear:

> Whereupon there rose a certaine crie of reioycing, not very great, done onely by a few, appointed for the purpose. But when Caesar refused the Diademe, then all the people together made an outcrie of ioy. Then Antonius offering it him againe, there was a second shout of ioy, but yet of a few. But when Caesar refused it againe the second time, then all the whole people shouted. Caesar hauing made this proofe, found that the people did not like of it and thereupon rose out of his chaire, and commanded the crowne to be caried vnto Iupiter in the Captioll (sig. 3R5v).

Plutarch's mixed judgment of Caesar is representative. "Perhaps more than any other figure in history," Ernest Schanzer sums, "Julius Caesar has evoked a divided response in the minds of those who have written about him."[3] Playwrights of Shakespeare's time testify to this. In France, a divided response to Caesar is seen in the plays of Muret (1553) and Grévin (1558), as well as in Grenier's *Cornelie* (1574), which Thomas Kyd, Shakespeare's contemporary, would later translate into English. But the force of Caesar in Shakespeare's day is undeniable. In his *Apology for Actors* (1612), Thomas Heywood tells of an actor overpowered by the part of Caesar, citing first Caesar's own theatricality.[4] Indeed, just a year before Shakespeare wrote *Julius Caesar*, his Chorus in *Henry V* praised Caesar's power and authority and hinted that Caesar might even save his country by analogizing him to the mistaken earl of Essex who, at first considered a hero, also sought the crown — in this case, of Elizabeth I herself:

But now behold,
In the quick forge and working-house of thought,
How London doth pour out her citizens!
The Mayor and all his brethren in best sort,
Like to the senators of th' antique Rome,
With the plebeians swarming at their heels,
Go forth and fetch their conqu'ring Caesar in,
As by a lower but by loving likelihood,
Were now the general of our gracious Empress,
As in good time he may, from Ireland coming,
Bringing a rebellion broached on his sword,
How many would the peaceful city quit,
To welcome him! (v.Chorus 22–34).

But Shakespeare was clearly entertaining doubts too. In *Julius Caesar*, Brutus cognitively transforms assassination into a holy sacrifice:

Let's kill him boldly, but not wrathfully;
Let's carve him as a dish fit for the gods,
Not hew him as a carcass fit for hounds (2.1.172–74)

and then turns the actual killing into a blood ritual:

Stoop, Romans, stoop,
And let us bathe our hands in Caesar's blood
Up to the elbows, and besmear our swords;

Then walk we forth, even to the market-place,
And waving our red weapons o'er our heads,
Let's all cry, "Peace, freedom, and liberty!" (3.1.105–10).

For Brutus, the power and authority the crown gives is frightening. In this, he echoes Christopher Marlowe's Theridimas: "A god is not so glorious as a king!" (*1 Tamburlaine*, 2.5.57).[5] Shakespeare's *Richard II* is also convinced of the absolute power the crown guarantees:

Not all the water in the rough rude sea
Can wash the balm from an anointed king;
The breath of worldly men cannot depose
The deputy elected by the Lord (*Richard II*, 3.2.55-58).

"Doth not the crown of England," echoes Shakespeare's King John, "prove the King?" (*King John*, 2.1.273). As for Shakespeare's early audiences, such beliefs find resonances in speeches and writings of King James, who likewise sees the divinity of kings. "Kings," James I says in a speech to the Lords and Commons of Parliament at Whitehall on March 21, 1610, "are iustly called Gods, for that they exercise a manner or resemblance of Diuine power vpon earth: For if you will consider the Attributes to God, you shall see how they agree in the person of a King. God hath power to create, or destroy, make, or vnmake at his pleasure, to giue life, or send death, to iudge all, and to bee iudged nor accomptable to none" (*Workes* [1616], sig. 2Y). In this James recalls Brutus' idea of Caesar. And James is also theatrical, like Antony. He writes in *Basilicon Doron, Or His Maiesties Instructions to His Dearest Sonne* (1598; 1603), "It is a trew old saying, That a King is as one set on a stage, whose smallest actions and gestures, all the people gazingly doe behold: and therefore although a King be neuer so praecise in the discharging of his Office, the people, who seeth but the outward part, will euer iudge of the substance, by the circumstances; and according to the outward appearance."[6] Cognitively, crowns carried inescapably forceful meanings in Shakespeare's theater, whether they were seen or not.

But the very fact that no crown is seen in *Julius Caesar* keeps its identity ambiguous. Plutarch calls the crown a laurel and a diadem; Casca thinks it was a coronet, and not a crown. But what it is that Caesar is being offered can cognitively change the meaning of the play and must, therefore, be identified in the mind's eye of each and every playgoer. The laurel wreath, for instance, was a fundamental Roman crown marking heroism, and it was well known in Shakespeare's day. It is what the military Titus Andronicus is awarded after a victory over the

Goths that features heavy losses (*Titus Andronicus* 1.1.74). *The Heroicall Devises* of Claudius Paradin, translated by P.S. in 1591, pictures the laurel and tells us in some detail what it signified to Shakespeare's culture. "The Romaines supposed it the chiefest reward of famous deedes, if they adorned their Emperors, captaines, knights, & other cōmon soldiers, euery one now withstāding according to their dignity, degree & place, with crownes or garlands, which they called militares coronas, martiall crownes, or crownes of chiualrie," he writes. It was thus a very special kind of crown that Plutarch is describing, one derived from heroic victory. It does not lead to absolutism, but to heroism as the basis for tribute and respect. "And because [the laurel crowns] were signes and tokens of their vertue, noble exploits, and inuincible minds," P.S. continues, "the chiefest and famoust had their portraitures, with their Apothegmes & posies, and that as well for the perpetuall remembrance of their worship, and ancientry as also for the oblectation, pleasure, & esperance to those that should come after, attending & feeling after the honor of vertue, with thereward & praise therof." They establish, preserve, or "redeem the common wealth."

Thus, the laurel crown historically signified not rule but military victory. "The first crowne that was giuen, was called triumphall, which being platted wt laurel bowes, and berries, was offered to inuincible triumphers. To whom it was lawfull, & that by the decree of the senate, to solemne their triumph vp and downe the cittie in great charets, and wagons, as vanquishers, and subduers of their enimies" — the remark resonates with the opening scene of Shakespeare's play where the

Figure 6: The Roman laurel wreath as *militare corona*, a martial crown

crowd comes to the Forum to welcome the conquering Caesar home: "the senate being aduertised first of 5000. Of their enimies to be slaine togither in one battel. Which triumphant crowne, in process of time, the Empire decreasing, was afterwards interlaced with vnions, and diuerse other precious stones. And last of all, it was changed from the naturall laurell, into a grauen laurell compassed about with a circle of gold, as is to be seene yet to this day in old coynes and pictures" (sigs. V3–V4). The laurel wreath — one of many deliberate possibilities for the unseen stage property cognitively dramatized in the mind's eye — has nothing to do with governance. In this sense, Brutus is horribly mistaken.

But North's Plutarch, translated under Elizabeth I, wavers, opening up various neural pathways in realizing this scene. The laurel crown may instead be a diadem, a very specific kind of crown. The regal diadem — an open band with several points — is what Elizabeth wore on the day before her coronation to signify limited sovereignty. As Elizabeth made her way through the streets of London, she met her own mirroring figure, her Cassius, in the person of Deborah, who, wearing a diadem herself, greeted the princess at the conduit in Fleet Street. In the day's pageantry, Deborah represented a powerful and godly woman and Elizabeth's chief biblical precedent for government by woman's rule (Judges 4–5), but Deborah was also dressed in robes described as a ruler's parliamentary attire, emphasizing Elizabeth's joint rule in and through the Houses of Lords and Commons. According to John N. King:

> Deborah in particular fuses the mediatory symbolism of medieval queens with the claim of kings to rule as divine agents or little "gods." The Hebrew prophetess, as the divinely inspired rescuer of Israel from Canaanite idolatry, is a figure for Elizabeth in the traditional regal role of intermediary between God and humanity rather than the queenly role of intercessor between king and people. This biblical device for government by woman recapitulates claims to providential governance by prophets that trace back to Moses.[7]

Deborah and the diadem she wears suggest limited (and shared) political power; as the official reporter Richard Mulcaster notes, the pageant means to suggest "that it behoveth both men and women so ruling to use advise of good counsell."[8] But as the biblical prototype, Deborah also underlined Elizabeth's attention to biblical and Reformist texts, and to the iconography of the New Jerusalem and the suffering of the elect, what King sees as "commonplace in Protestant Europe," although "only in England did they focus on biblical women as bearers of salvation" (p. 227). The tableau with Deborah was also associated with a previous tableau in the Queen's royal passage through the city in which a Protestant figure of Truth appropriated the motto of Elizabeth's late Catholic sister Queen Mary Tudor, whose motto had been *Veritas Temporis Filia* (Truth is the daughter of Time). Furthermore, a masque at the Little Conduit in Cheapside displayed two hills, one "cragged, barreyn, and stonye" and the other "fayre, fresh, grene and beawtifull." The first was labelled *Ruinosa Respublica* as the state of the commonwealth under the Catholic Mary and the second signifying *Respublica bene instituta*, the good republic to be established under Elizabeth's Protestant faith. Between the two hills was a cave in which Father Time lived and from which he led Veritas, his daughter. The girl presented Elizabeth with a copy of the English Bible or "*Verbum veritatis*, the woorde of trueth."[9] Figuring Truth, the girl, clad in white silk, would also come in time to figure the baby Elizabeth in Shakespeare and Fletcher's *Henry VIII; or All Is True*, where Archbishop Cranmer prophesies, "Truth shall nurse her, Holy and heavenly thoughts still counsel her" (5.4.28–29). Deborah with her diadem as a mirroring prototype also underscored Elizabeth's concerns for her people. As Richard Grafton writes in his *Abridgement of the Chronicles of England* (1570), Deborah's presence was meant "to encourage the Queene not to feare though shee were a woman. For women by the Spirite and power of almightie God, have ruled both honorably and politiquely" (sig. Z3).[10] If the Elizabethan play of *Julius Caesar* recalls Elizabeth's rule and her diadem, then Brutus' silent accusations of Caesar are far wide of the mark, and his own ambition to climb, and his own jealousy of Caesar's power and popularity, cause him to bring down a ruler whose authority could harbor negotiations with the Senate and peace for an exhausted Rome. The ghost Brutus sees at Philippi is quite right: "the gods were offended with the murther of Caesar," as Plutarch has it. As the Herald tells Edward II in Christopher Marlowe's play, the "brightness" of Caesar's diadem is something that only "pernicious upstarts" such as Brutus can "dim" (*Edward II*, 3.1.164–65).[11]

Other crowns on the stages of Shakespeare's time carried with them this same notion of honorable, conciliatory, and limited rule. Brutus tells Locrine in W.S.'s *The Lamentable Tragedie of Locrine* (1595), "For thou must beare the person of a King." Placing the crown on his head, he continues, "Stand vp, and weare the regall Crowne, And thinke vpon the state of Maiestie, That thou with honor well maist weare the crown" (1.1.187–91).[12] "Tis you are in possession of the Crowne," Phillip, duke of Lorraine, tells his father King John of France, in the anonymous *Raigne of King Edward the Third* (1596), "And thats the surest poynt of all the Law" (3.1.109-10).[13]

But royal law could be redefined. In *The Trew Law of Free Monarchies: Or the Reciprock and Mvtvall Dvetie Betwixt a Free King, and His Naturall Subiects* by James I, which went through one edition in 1598 and two more on his coronation in England in 1603, the title promises the mediation of a ruler of limited power. But the text that follows features a crown far more powerful than the diadem:

> The Kings ... in Scotland were before any estates or rankes of men within the same, before any Parliaments were holden, or lawes made: and by them was the land distributed (which at the first was whole theirs) states erected and decerned, and formes of gouernement deuised and established. And so it followes of necessitie, that the kings were the authors and makers of the Lawes, and not the Lawes of the kings (sig. R5).

Thus, "ye see it manifest, that the King is ouer-Lord of the whole land so is he Master ouer euery person that inhabiteth the same, hauing power ouer the life and death of euery one of them" (sig. R6). James seeks support for this extension of royal power in natural law.

> And the proper office of a King towards his Subiects, agrees very wel with the office of the head towards the body, and all members thereof: For from the head, being the seate of Iudgement, proceedeth the care and foresight of guiding, and preuenting all euill that may come to the body or any part thereof. The head cares for the body, so doeth the King for his people. . . . And for the similitude of the head and the body, it may very well fall out that the head will be forced to garre cut off some rotten member (as I haue already said) to keepe the rest of the body in integritie: but what state the body can be in, if the head, for any infirmitie that can fall to it, be cut off, I leaue it to the readers iudgement (sigs. R6v, S1).

And if the argument is raised that a wicked man may become king or tyrant, then that, James continues, is as it should be:

> Whereunto for answer, I grant indeed, that a wicked king is sent by God for a curse to his people, and a plague for their sinnes: but that it is lawfull to them to shake off that curse at their owne

> hand, which God hath laid on them, that I deny, and may so do iustly (*Workes*, sig. S1v).

James's definition of the crown is not that of the diadem, but another recognition altogether. In Shakespeare's *Tragedy of Richard III*, Queen Elizabeth anticipates Brutus' suspicions when she asks Richard:

> Hid'st thou that forehead with a golden crown
> Where should be branded, if that right were right,
> The slaughter of the prince that ow'd that crown,
> And the dire death of my poor sons and brothers? (*Richard III*, 4.4.140–43).

And her fears of Richard, and Brutus' of Caesar, with their crowns, may be justified. For earlier, Richard II has told Northumberland:

> Your children yet unborn and unbegot,
> That lift your vassal hands against my head,
> And threat the glory of my precious crown
> Tell Bullingbrook — for yon methinks he stands —
> That every stride he makes upon my land
> Is dangerous treason. He is come to open
> The purple testament of bleeding war;
> But ere the crown he looks for live in peace,
> Ten thousand bloody crowns of mothers' sons
> Shall ill become the flower of England's face,
> Change the complexion of her maid-pale peace
> To scarlet indignation, and bedew
> Her pasters' grass with faithful English blood. (*Richard II*, 3.3.88–100).

A king's absolute power as theorized by James I and ascribed to Caesar by Brutus and his fellow conspirators is further theorized at length by the Machiavellian Duke of Guise in Marlowe's *Massacre at Paris*:

> Oft have I levelled, and at last have learned
> That peril is the chiefest happiness,
> And resolution honour's fairest aim....
> And thereon set the diadem of France,
> I'll either rend it with my nails to naught,
> Or mount the top with my aspiring wings,
> Although my downfall be the deepest hell. ...

As Caesar to his soldiers, so say I:
Those that hate me will I learn to loathe.
Give me a look that, when I bend the brows
Pale death may walk in furrows of my face;
A hand that with a grasp may gripe the world;
An ear to hear what my detractors say;
A royal seat, a sceptre, and a crown;
That those which do behold, they may become
As men that stand and gaze against the sun. (scene 2, 34–36; 41–44; 95–103).[14]

But the burden of rule epitomized in an unseen crown — its temptations, its dangers, and its consequences, all of which Brutus seems to overlook — were also universally acknowledged. The Ghost of Hamlet tells his son of the dangers awaiting a king:

Now, Hamlet, hear:
'Tis given out that, sleeping in my orchard,
A serpent stung me, so the whole ear of Denmark
Is by a forged process of my death
Rankly abus'd (1.5.34–38).

But the murderer Claudius rests no easier:

My fault is past, but, O, what form of prayer
Can serve my turn? "Forgive me my foul murther"?
That cannot be, since I am still possess'd
Of those effects for which I did the murther:
My crown, mine own ambition, and my queen (*Hamlet*, 3.3.51–55).

For the abandoned York, the crown is a mockery made of paper (*3 Henry VI*, 1.4.96 s.d.). Macbeth traces the trajectory of his assassination of Duncan from his first conscious inkling — "If chance will have me king, why chance may crown me" (1.3.143) — to the recognition of its emptiness:

Upon my head they plac'd a fruitless crown,
And put a barren sceptre in my gripe,
Thence to be wrench'd with an unlineal hand,
No son of mine succeeding (3.1.60-63)

— to ongoing punishment: "Thy crown does sear mine eyeballs" (4.1.113). Leontes, too, knows horror in *The Winter's Tale*: " I have drunk, and seen the spider," he says, fearing "There is a plot against my life, my crown, All's true that is mistrusted" (2.1.45–47). Richard II makes Bullingbrook's usurpation visible in the struggle he undergoes with Bullingbrook on stage to take the crown. The crown that passes to Bullingbrook does not fare so well in *King Lear* (1.1) but here the crown is not a crown but a coronet.

Coronets — another cognitive speculation that Plutrarch first provides concerning Caesar's crown — were first introduced in the reign of Richard II; they were worn by dukes, not kings, so that Lear is either confused in his division of the kingdom or deliberately keeping Cornwall and Albany at a restricted level of authority: if he is thus withholding his final surrender of power, he may be testing what kind of rule will succeed his own. Although coronets briefly disappeared in Elizabethan England with the death of her last duke, the duke of Norfolk in 1571, they were reintroduced in the reign of James. But as Andrew Gurr has noted, by emphasizing coronets rather than crowns — through a staged displacement of authority — Albany has only a coronet to offer at the play's end and only two earls to whom he may pass it on. The end of *King Lear* thus turns on how the coronet itself is staged, as Gurr has remarked:

> The presence of Albany's coronet as a feature of the play's closure leaves us with not just two possible and alternative resolutions to the play but four.
>
> If at the Court performance in 1606 Edgar was left with the coronet in his hands or on his head, such a posture would look very different from the later [folio text], since the earlier [quarto] gives the last speech to Albany, while the Folio allocated it to Edgar. The last four ponderous lines sound quite different if delivered by a coronet-wearing Albany. They are different again if given by Albany while Edgar holds the coronet, and even more different if delivered by Edgar without the golden headgear. The fourth option, Edgar speaking while holding the coronet, is the only choice possible for those who need to see some expression of hope for the future expressed by a single and fully comprehending speaker in the last speech.[15]

In any event, the transfer of power is curtailed, as Prospero points out in his account to Miranda in *The Tempest*; the frustrated Antonio thought him:

now incapable; confederates
(So dry he was for sway) wi' th' King of Naples,
To give him annual tribute, do him homage,
Subject his coronet to his crown, and bend
The dukedom yet unbow'd (alas, poor Milan!)
To most ignoble stooping (1.2.111–16).

For Shakespeare's playgoers, then, Antony's offering Caesar a crown and not a coronet might convey in later productions the absolute power James would authorize and promulgate, rather than the limited power promulgated by Elizabeth's staged doctrine.

There is good reason, then, for Brutus to be apprehensive, and in a way that must have been especially pointed at early performances of *Julius Caesar.* At the battle of Runnymede in the thirteenth century, a body of powerful English nobility forced King John to acknowledge in the *Magna Carta* that the supremacy of the monarch was conditional, creating the basis for the "mixed monarchy" of Shakespeare's England in which authority was theoretically held and exercised by the monarch along with the two houses of Parliament. When power shifted to the monarch and a group of loyal members of the aristocracy under the Tudors, Commons grew increasingly restless. By 1610 a Puritan faction had so increased its strength that Commons declared that the English government ought to be described as "King-in-Parliament." Their sense of James's understanding of rule as absolutist parallels Brutus' uneasy thoughts about Caesar's unchecked ambition. Quite apart from personal motivations, conscious or not, Brutus thinks that the power of the crown will transfer authority from the Senate to the sovereign and fundamentally transform the political nature of Rome. Such a change will not only undo the relationship between law and rule; it also has the force of transforming the character of the ruler himself: "He would be crown'd: How that might change his nature, there's the question" (2,1,12–13). Brutus thus champions limited monarchy, precisely the cause of the increasingly influential forces of resistance under Elizabeth, following the Scot George Buchanan, James's own boyhood tutor, who argued in his *De Jure Regni apud Scotus dialogus* (1570) that rulers must be constrained "to make use not of their own licentious wills in judgement, but of that right or privilege which the People had conferred upon them."[16] For Buchanan and his followers, the menace of an absolute dictator — the title Plutarch tells us the people had twice given Caesar at this point — would work in opposition to the common good. Such a risk of tyranny could doom a commonwealth.

But by 1606, Macbeth's "imperial theme" (1.3.129) — what Brutus fears — had become Malcolm's "imperial charge" (4.3.20) — what Brutus foresees. Empire was not a new concept; what Caesar stands for was commonplace to Tudor thought and sensibility. The preamble to Henry VIII's *Act in Restraint of Appeals* (1533) lay claim to "this realm of England [as] an empire,"[18] and his title made him King of England, Ireland, and France. Henry did not wear a diadem, much less a coronet. He wore the larger, enclosed imperial crown, opening up a whole new path for cognitive speculation. Henry VIII's easy assumption of empire is displayed in the 1547 draft of his will, in which he wrote "a full and plain gift disposition assignement declaration limitation and appoinctment wt' what conditions our doughters Mary and Elizabeth shall severally have hold and enjoye the sayd imperial Crowne and other the premiss's after our deceasse and for default of issue and heyres of the severall bodyes of us and of our sonne prince Edward lawfully begotten and his heyres."[19] Indeed, the first edition of John Foxe's *Actes and Monuments* (1563) compares the early sufferings of Elizabeth I with the Marian persecution of Reformed martyrs and her reign to that of Constantine, the Church's first emperor; he made the assignment emblematic by placing her portrait within the capital *C* of Constantine. But many of the official portraits of the Queen, such as the engravings on the title pages of the Bishop's Bible (1569) and Christopher Saxton's *Atlas of England and Wales* (1579) where she is seen as "a patron of geography," writes Stephen Orgel, "makes an imperial claim."[20] Under Elizabeth, New World exploration was increased, while piracy on the high seas attempted to intercept and weaken Spanish ships. "In Crispin van de Passe's 1596 engraving of the queen," Orgel continues:

> Elizabeth stands between the pillars of Hercules, originally devised as an impresa of the [Holy Roman Emperor] Charles V, and signifying his determination to sail "Plus Ultra," to retake the Holy Land and expand his empire beyond the boundaries of Europe; it subsequently became the *impresa* of his son Philip II of Spain, the husband of Elizabeth's Catholic half-sister Mary Tudor, and the first of her suitors after she herself became queen. The Queen's image, with its naval background, not only celebrates the maritime victory over her brother-in-law in 1588, and the more recent naval triumph at Cadiz, but at a time when the exploration and colonization of the New World were starting to be a critical element in English political life, asserts Elizabeth's own imperial claims (pp. 119-21).

Figure 7: Elizabeth I as Emperor Constantine from John Foxe, *Actes and Monuments* (1563)

The stage prototype of imperialism was Marlowe's Tamburlaine. According to Techelles,

> As princely lions when they rouse themselves,
> Stretching their paws, and threat'ning herds of beasts,
> So in his armor looketh Tamburlaine,
> Methinks I see kings kneeling at his feet,
> And he, with frowning brows and fiery looks,
> Spurning their crowns from off their captive heads (*1 Tamburlaine*, 1.2.52–57).

"Reioyce, my Lord," the Herald announces at the close of the anonymous play of *The Reigne of King Edward III*,

ascend the imperial throne!
The mightie and redoubted prince of Wales,
Great seruitor to bloudie Mars in armes,
The French mans terror, and his countries fame,
Triumphant rideth like a Romane peere (5.1.176-80).

Shakespeare's Prince Hal is similarly attracted: "My due from thee is this imperial crown," he tells his father, "Which as immediate from thy place and blood, Derives itself to me" (*2 Henry IV*, 4.5.41–43); it becomes a joyous battle cry in *Henry V* when an exuberant Chorus exclaims,

Now all the youth of England are on fire. ...
For now sits Expectation in the air,
And hides a sword, from hilts unto the point,
With crown imperial, crowns, and coronets,
Promis'd to Harry and his followers (3.Chr.1; 8-11).

The basis for Henry VIII's expropriation of the title of King of France is at hand.

The Stuart line followed the Tudor introduction of imperialism. When James passed under the seven memorial arches in his own royal entry into London in 1603, the first arch was designed by Ben Jonson with a figure representing the monarchy of Britain sitting below the crowns of England and Scotland with the motto, "Orbis Britannicus, Divisus ab orbe," which, Jonson said, was "to shew that this empire is a world divided from the world." He was referring to James as Augustus, making a direct link to the Roman Caesars.[21] John Russell wrote a treatise called "the happie and blissed Unioun betuixt the tua ancienne realmes of Scotland and Ingland ... presently undir the gratious monarchie and impyir of our dread soveraine, King James the Sixt of Scotland, First of Ingland, France and Ireland," and James was given an accession medal that read "Emperor of the whole island of Britain." His appeal to Rome, following that of Elizabeth but more pronounced, led to a rash of Roman plays — *Sejanus, Cataline His Conspiracy, Antony and Cleopatra*, and *Coriolanus* among them. But James pursued his own agenda of imperialism too in his desire to unite Scotland and England to form what he coined as "Great Britain." He used the imperial crown wherever possible — in speeches, proclamations, and documents — where it often replaces the diadem or royal crown, and on the most significant proclamations it appears just above "By the King," or, in the case of the proclamation on the Gunpowder Plot, actually replaces those words.

Figure 8: Title page of the Bishop's Bible (1569) showing Justice and Mercy placing the imperial crown on Elizabeth I

In an inventory of 1606, James records,

> The Imperiall Diadem and Crowne, and other Roiall and Princely ornaments and Jewells to be indyvidually and inseparably for ever hereafter annexed to the Kingdome of this Realm.
>
> Imprimis, the Imperiall Crowne of this Realme, of gould, the border garnished with seaven ballaces, eight saphiers, five pointed diamonds, twenty rubies (two of them being craised [broken]), nineteen pearles, and one of the crosses of the same Crown garnished with a great sapphire, an emoralde crased, four ballaces and nyne pearles not all of one sort.[22]

As Augustus, known for his learning, and as Emperor, known for his widespread rule, James was the double heir of the Roman Caesars, a descendant of the Octavius Caesar of Shakespeare's play who is part of the triumvirate that takes power (by defeating Brutus and Cassius)

Figure 9: Title page of Christopher Saxton, *Atlas of England and Wales* (1579), showing Elizabeth I as an imperial ruler in her own right

after the assassination of Julius Caesar. Henslowe's property list for the Lord Admiral's Men includes "three Imperial crowns, one plain crown [the diadem], one ghost's crown; one crown with a sun."[23] This number of imperial crowns may suggest the centrality of imperialist thought and behavior to the drama of Shakespeare's time, but it does not tell us how the playwrights and their audiences felt about imperialism. It does not tell us whether this became an unusually worn cognitive pathway. James's increasingly absolutist thoughts and actions find ready response in the subversive plots of Jonson's two Roman tragedies, growing Puritan opposition to James's rule, and a general displeasure with James's personality. Francis Bacon ends his essay "Of Empire" by concluding that "All precepts concernng Kinges are in effect comprehended in these two remembrances. *Memento quod es homo* and *Memento quo es Deus* or *Vice dei*: The one to bridle their [imperialist] power, & the other their will" (1612 edition, sig. I8v). This is a reference, according to Ernst H. Kantorowicz, to the new Roman emperor, on route to the Capitol, who is told by his slave, "Look behind thee. Remember thou art a man."[24] Brutus' attempt to curtail Caesar could be as telling in a performance of *Julius Caesar* as the emperor's meteoric rise to imperial power, to the title of perpetual dictator.

Yet Shakespeare supplied playgoers with still another kind of crown — and the one they saw and heard about most often, the crown of thorns. An important religious affiliation between the royal sovereign and religion is seen with Elizabeth when Foxe pictured her within the capital *C* of Constantine in his *Actes and Monuments*. She is pictured with a defeated pope entwined with demonic serpents beneath her feet. In this prominent (and propagandistic) engraving, "The heaviness of the queen's dais bears down the pontiff [seen on the lower left rim of the letter], whose tiara and broken keys are 'outweighed' spiritually by her regalia, the royal arms, and Tudor roses," John N. King notes:

> The cornucopia integrated with the head of the *C* symbolizes her reign as a time of peaceful "harvest" following spiritual discord; the horn of plenty had long been used as an attribute of a fruitfulness and concord. … The figure of the queen assimilates overlapping images of the Coronation of the Virgin and the Blessed Virgin's trampling of symbols of evil. … All of this is explicit, but the woodcut may also redefine long-established imagery of the Adoration of the Magi by placing three men who reenact the homage of the Three Kings in the favored position at the queen's right-hand side (pp. 155–56).

Eliza Triumphans, an engraving by William Rogers (1589) to celebrate the defeat of the Spanish Armada, shows Elizabeth with a crown combining the circlets of palm and oak leaves proffered by personifications of women to form the triple crown of empire, but this picture, says King, "may also preserve a remote parody of the tiara toppled from the pope's head in so many allegorical portraits of the Tudors" (p. 242). In his poem *Elizabetha Triumphes* (1588), James Aske tells of "damned practizes, that the divelish Popes of Rome have used ever sithence her Highness first comming to the Crowne, by moving her wicked and traiterous subjects to Rebellion and conspiracies"; his work consistently opposed the Queen and the pope. In *The Triplicitie of Triumphes* (1591), Lodowick Lloyud parodies the papal tiara with an intricate pattern of threes pertaining to the Queen: her birthday on September 7, her Accession Day on November 17, and her coronation on January 15.[25] Such opposition raises the imperial crown of Caesar to nearly a salvational level, suggesting that the conspirators in *Julius Caesar* are members of the devil's party — wicked, destructive, sinful. Foxe had gone further —

> Finally, the crowne of Christ was of sharpe thorne; the Pope hath three crownes of gold upon hys head, so far excedying Christ the sonne of God in glory of this world, as Christ excedeth hym in the glory of heaven[26] —

suggesting opposition to the papacy as a kind of martyrdom. It was an image that held great appeal for King James:

> One day reading privatly to my selfe the passion of Christ, in the end of S. Matthewes Gospell, I lighted upon that part, where the Governors Souldiers mocked our Saviour, with putting the ornaments of A King upon him. Which appeared to me to be so punctually set doune, that my head hammered upon it divers times after, and specially the Croune of thornes went never out of my mind, remembering the thorny cares, which a King (if he have a care of his office) must be subject unto, as (God knowes) I daily and nightly feele in my owne person. …
>
> Out of our owne predecessours, Henrie the fourth … being in a traunce upon his death-bed; his sonne, Henrie the fift, thinking he had beene dead, a little too nimbly carried away the croune that stood by his Father: but the King recovering a little out of his fit missed his croune, and called for it; and when his sonne brought it backe againe, hee tolde him that, if hee had

> knowen what a croune was, hee would not have been so hastie; for hee protested that hee was never a day without trouble since it was first put upon his head [cf. *2 Henry IV*, 4.5.23–25].

This is a very different James from the imperialist theoretician and ruler of his earlier years; his self-recognition seems to have changed, at least outwardly. In James's *Meditation upon the 27, 28, 29 Verses of the XXVIIth Chapter of Saint Matthew, or A Paterne for a Kings Inauguration* (1619) for his son Charles, he enlarges on his understanding of the crown of thorns, now derived from the word diadem — what Plutarch says Antony offered to Caesar.

> As to the stuffe wherof this Croune was made, it was made of thornes: and it is vulgarly well knowen that thornes signifie stinging and pricking cares. That King, therefore, who will take his paterne from this heavenly King must not thinke to weare a Croune of gold and precious stones only, but it must be lyned with Thornes, that is, thornie cares: for he must remember that he weares not that croune for himselfe, but for others; that hee is ordayned for his people, and not his people for him. For he is a great watchman and shepheard, as well as Church-men are: and his eye must never slumber nor sleepe for the care of his flocke, ever remembering that his office, beeing duely executed, will prove as much onus as honos unto him. And as to the forme of making the croune of thornes, it is said, they platted thornes and made a croune of them. Now every man knoweth, that where a number of long things, in forme of lines, shall be platted through other, it makes a troublesome and intricate worke to find out all the ends of them, and set them asunder againe, especially to set straight and eaven againe all the severall peeces that must be bowed in the platting: but above all, to set straight and asunder againe thornes that are platted, is a most uncomfortable worke. For though any one peece of thorne may be handled in some place without hurt, yet no man can touch platted thornes without danger of pricking.[27]

Although James presents this idea as his own, there were in fact crowns made with intertwined thorns of metal worked into them. They are pictured and discussed at great length in the *Symbola Politica* of Diego de Saavedra Fajardo (1640), published in Spanish followed by Latin, Italian, and German texts. "Crowns have cares" was a Tudor proverb, appearing in George Pettie's *Petite Pallace of Pettie his Pleasure* in 1576 (I, 101; II,136),

Figure 10: The monarch's crown with thorns, from Saavedra Fajardo, *Symbola Christiano-Politica* (1569)

but also, among other places, in Thomas Lodge's novel *Rosalynde* in 1590 (p. 28); the anonymous romance *Selimus* in 1594 (sig. A3v); and in Samuel Daniel's play *Philotas* in 1605 (2.3). At the point of his own death, King Charles remembered his father's words in the *Eikon Basilike* (1640):

> I would rather choose to wear a crown of thorns with my Saviour, than to exchange that of gold, which is due to me, for one of lead, whose embased flexibleness shall be forced to bend and comply to the various and oft contrary dictates of any factions, when instead of reason and public concernments they obtrude nothing but what makes for the interest of parties, and flows from the partialities of private wills and passions. (28)

Both James and Charles knew the cares of the crown; both seem comfortable with comparing their lot to that of Christ. The role of mediator, of peacekeeper, for them was not only desirable but crucial. This too has its cognitive pathways to Shakespeare's *Julius Caesar*. By assassinating the one man who can organize and sustain the social and political fabric of Brutus' Rome, the conspirators provoke factionalism and seemingly unending bloodshed. The conspirators, warns Antony, "let slip the dogs of war, That this foul deed [the assassination] shall smell above the earth With carrion men, groaning for burial" (3.1.273–75). The situation is made unbearably real in the death of Cinna the poet (3.3.27–38); "Tear him to pieces" (3.3.28; 30). "O, when degree is shak'd," Ulysses reminds playgoers in *Troilus and Cressida*,

> Which is the ladder of all high designs,
> The enterprise is sick. How could communities,
> Degrees in schools, and brotherhoods in cities,
> Peaceful commerce from dividable shores,
> The primogenity and due of birth,
> Prerogative of age, crowns, sceptres, laurels,
> But by degree stand in authentic place? (1.3.101–08).

The political alliances swirling around the unseen crown in *Julius Caesar* were so contemporary to Shakespeare's own audiences that no playgoer could feel excused from his own cognitive allegiances, his own recognition of right rule, of political stability, of the future of the state. Choosing the right kind of crown, then — coronet or diadem, imperial crown or a crown of thorns — as the focus of the mind's eye is vital and unavoidable. We dare not choose the wrong option. Betrayed by the battlefield misunderstanding of Cassius, Titinius cries out, "Alas, thou has misconstrued everything" (5.3.84). Playgoers construing advisedly their need to interpret the offstage crown that Antony would place on the head of Caesar do so at their own peril.

SHAKESPEARE'S RINGS

Contrary to his power and effect in *The Merchant of Venice*, Shylock has only five scenes and 357 lines. The pivotal scene is 3.1 where, in rapid succession, Salerio and Solanio confirm Jessica's departure, Shylock delivers a curse on her as dreadful as Lear will place on his two elder daughters, and, with Tubal's help, he closes a brief scene of 130 lines swearing to have the heart of Antonio. His forceful, jagged bursts of language, alternating between shock and despair, seem confused; at times, he seems to speak at cross-purposes. But this is not so. The linguist Charles J. Fillmore says that even the most disparate words at a given moment are deeply associated by what he calls "semantic frames."[1] Reviled, mocked, humiliated, Shylock knows precisely the semantic frame of his tumbling, tumultuous reactions: "I am a Jew" (3.1.58). Although his remarks and reactions take many forms in this highly charged scene, he fiercely holds to this premise. It explains all that he thinks, says, and does, yet by the end of this compressed scene it also undoes him.

He enters at line 22 to Solanio's taunting: "How, now, Shylock, what news among the merchants?" (3.1.22–23). Shylock seems not to hear him, for his reply has nothing at all to do with merchants, merchandise, or bonds. He speaks instead of what is obsessing him: "You know, none so well, none so well as you, of my daughter's flight" (24–25). They agree, and he interprets its significance. "She is damn'd for it" (31). She is damned because she has denied her own Jewish heritage for a Christian. Now Solanio jokes. But Shylock's mind is fixated on Jessica's spiritual condition—and his own: "My flesh and blood to rebel!" (34). The rebellion, once tribal, is now familial, of his own bloodline. Again there is mockery, and again he works out the consequences quite apart from them: "I say, my daughter is my flesh and my blood." (37–38) Now he too is deeply implicated. Her damnation endangers his own. She is his entire family; he is both mother and father to her. She represents the crux of his family; Shakespeare seems to know that the Jewish lineage, unlike his own, passes down through the female line, and for Shylock, she has damned that lineage forever.

Salerio, shallow as always, talks past Shylock, does not perceive his train of thought:

> There is more difference between thy flesh and hers than between jet and ivory, more between your bloods than there is between red wine and Rhenish. But tell us, do you hear whether Antonio have had any loss at sea or no?" (39–42).

Shylock's answer—"There I have another bad match" (44)—seems, on the surface, to change the subject agreeably; but in fact he is making a comparison between Antonio and himself by fixating on the idea of loss. For a moment he verbalizes the comparison—"A bankrout, a prodigal, who dares scarce show his head on the Rialto" (44–46), but then he moves on to distinguish Antonio from his daughter—from his flesh and his blood—by holding him to account where he can no longer hold his daughter to hers. By making Antonio the alien culture, his mind struggles to define just what it could be that seduced Jessica, to define that community to which she now subscribes, in an attempt to understand her, to understand her action, and, quite possibly, to comprehend her "damnation." The famous declarations that follow, in the speech beginning "I am a Jew," however, are anything but the declarations they are most often taken for:

> I am a Jew. Hath not a Jew eyes? Hath not a Jew hands, organs, dimensions, senses, affections, passions; fed with the same food, hurt with the same weapons, subject to the same diseases, heal'd by the same means, warm'd and cool'd by the same winter and summer, as a Christian is? If you prick us, do we not bleed? If you tickle us, do we not laugh? If you poison us, do we not die? And if you wrong us, shall we not revenge? If we are like you in the rest, we will resemble you in that. If a Jew wrong a Christian, what is his humility? Revenge. If a Christian wrong a Jew, what should his sufferance be by Christian example? Why, revenge.

> The villany you teach me, I will execute, and it shall go hard but I will better the instruction (58–73).

This is a deeply disturbing speech because Shylock does not want to be like a Christian—Shylock is a Jew—and he is anxiously searching for what it is that differentiates, rather than assimilates, their cultures. He must determine that to determine why Jessica was so attracted to Christians. He is *not* struggling to show common humanity with Christians for he thinks there is none, but he *is* struggling to reestablish what it means to be a Jew and therefore *not* a Christian. It is difficult for him, and he takes refuge in "if." That set of hypotheses will save him from any danger of assimilation. His tattered logic is the logic of grief.

When Antonio calls away Salerio and Solanio and Tubal arrives, Shylock, still dwelling on the loss of his daughter—the end of his family line—demands of his friend whether his family can in fact be reconstituted: "How now, Tubal, what news from Genoa? Hast thou found my daughter?" (79–80). This is a significant variation on the question he had asked of Salerio and Solanio, because this time he is addressing a fellow Jew. Tubal's reply—"I often came where I did hear of her, but cannot find her" (81–82)—is now the heaviest burden of all. Now she is no longer lost just to Shylock; she is lost to their tribe. She is no longer one of them; she is no longer a Jew. Shylock's dreadful curse on her follows as if to seal this last recognition, for any hypothetical reversal of fortune, any hope for a second conversion, is now gone. Just as Shylock's brain had used "I am a Jew" as an unconscious semantic frame to hold together the various scraps of news, so now this fragile cognitive process gives way to uncontrolled grief and, although for a fleeting second he sees Jessica's betrayal as a betrayal of their nation, he surrounds this, first and last, by the painful acknowledgement that it is a betrayal of their family, and of him.

> Why, there, there, there, there! A diamond gone, cost me two thousand ducats in Frankford! The curse never fell upon our nation till now, I never felt it till now. Two thousand ducats in that, and other precious, precious jewels. I would my daughter were dead at my foot, and the jewels in her ear! Would she were hears'd at my foot, and the ducats in her coffin! No news of them? Why, so—and I know not what's spent in the search. Why, thou loss upon loss! the thief gone with so much to find the thiefs, and no satisfaction, no revenge, nor no ill luck stirring but what lights a' my shoulders, no sighs but a' my breathing, no tears but a' my shedding (83–96).

That he would not take back the jewels and ducats but bury them with her is telling—for he is speaking here of the family legacy: when Jessica is gone, all he has accumulated to establish a family legacy is gone; without an agent, the material goods are worth nothing. She, it seems, had been in that sense worth everything to him.

The brain scientist John J. Ratney suggests what is happening here:

> Most incoming sensory information is sent first to the thalamus, which then relays it to the sensory and frontal lobes for detailed analysis and response. But when emotionally charged information comes in, the thalamus sends it on a more rapid pathway to the amygdala, bypassing the upper brain's input since there is no time to think about how to respond. Based on the limited memory information it has received, the amygdala uses primitive, general categorizations—primary emotions—to activate an immediate aggressive or defensive response. Specialized cortical networks in the right hemisphere and frontal lobes are responsible for secondary emotions and modulating the more primal emotional responses of the amygdala and the limbic system.[2]

The aggression comes in the imaged curse—the coffin, the body, the jewels—and the defense in the totality of that image: not simply Jessica, but all that remains are the proper subjects for burial. Both his heir and her inheritance are gone and he will seal their departure permanently together. This exercise of unfathomable grief is also a consequence of his controlling semantic frame.

So far, Shylock's scattered responses and conflicting remarks all share a common source. But Tubal has more news from Genoa. Antonio has lost an argosy coming from Tripolis. ("I thank God, I thank God. Is it true, is it true?" 102–03). In one night in Genoa Jessica spent fourscore ducats. ("Thou stick'st a dagger in me. I shall never see my gold again"); Tubal has confirmed his curse and made her the cause of that action (111–12). Antonio's creditors have come to Venice to break him.

Shylock: I am very glad of it. I'll plague him, I'll torture him. I am glad of it.
Tubal: One of them show'd me a ring that he had of your daughter for a monkey.
Shylock: Out upon her! Thou torturest me, Tubal. It was my turkis, I had it of Leah when I was a bachelor. I would not have given it for a wilderness of monkeys (116–23).

This is the last and the most telling blow to Shylock. Leah's ring was traded for a monkey. That very act, by itself, causes Shylock to change from acknowledging Antonio's downfall to actively pursuing it. ("Go, Tubal, fee me an officer" 125–26). For Jessica, Leah's turquoise ring was presumably just one more jewel stolen from her father when eloping with Lorenzo. But for Shylock, the ring represents the sacred bond between wife and husband, a holy relic uniting Jessica's mother and father that she has exchanged for a pet that emblematically signifies unruled lechery. Imaging the coffin, pronouncing Jessica dead had been for Shylock a kind of closure. Now Tubal reminds him that the debt Antonio owes Shylock still entangles the two communities. The Christians who invaded Shylock's house are still bonded to him through Antonio's unpaid loan. Clearly, what turns Shylock's obsessive attention from the loss of Jessica to revenge on Antonio is the loss of Leah's gift ring. But just what kind of ring was it, and what is its overpowering talismanic force? Why does that single ring outweigh all the other jewelry—and Jessica as well? What is its cognitive power?

Leah's ring is not the only ring implicated in this conversation, and Shylock's neglect of another ring is also cognitively significant. That is the seal ring or signet ring, a finger-ring that had a die with a raised or incised emblematic design, letter, word, or sentence that was used to stamp an impression on a plastic substance such as wax, often adhering to, or attached by cords or parchment slips to, a document of legal attestation. This guarantee of authority is what first sealed the relationship between Shylock and Antonio, when Antonio promised to "seal unto [our] bond" and Shylock replied, "Then meet me forthwith at the notary's" (1.3.171–72). The merchant Simon Eyre uses his seal ring to authorize Firk to buy him a braided gown and a damask cassock in Thomas Dekker's *Shoemakers' Holiday* (scene vii, 124–25).[3] The necessity of sealing documents this way to complete and secure them was practiced at the highest levels of Elizabethan government. The Lord Keeper of the Great Seal—Sir Thomas Egerton at the time of this play—was the second-ranking state officer and he affixed the seal to all proclamations, writs, letters patent, and documents giving power to sign and to ratify treaties under Elizabeth; at times, the office was combined with that of Lord Chancellor. The Lord Keeper of the Privy Seal—William Cecil, first Lord Burghley under Elizabeth at the time—was the fourth-ranking officer of state and used the seal whenever the Great Seal was unavailable and, increasingly in Elizabethan times, for financial payments as a warrant from the Exchequer. Shakespeare is well aware of this when Archbishop Cranmer indicates royal support by carrying the King's own ring into a meeting of the Privy Council, where they revile him in the final act of *Henry VIII or All Is True*:

Cranmer: Must I go like a traitor thither?
Bishop Gardiner: Receive him,
And see him safe i' th' Tower.
Cranmer: Stay, good my lords,
I have a little yet to say. Look there, my lords;
By virtue of that ring, I take my cause
Out of the gripes of cruel men, and give it
To a most noble judge, the King my master.
Lord Chamberlain: This is the King's ring.
Earl of Surrey: 'Tis no counterfeit.
Earl of Suffolk: 'Tis the right ring, by heav'n! I told ye all,
When we first put this dangerous stone a-rolling,
'Twould fall upon ourselves (5.2.131–41).

But such signet rings were used at all levels of society. Shakespeare himself when writing (or dictating) his will "have her[e]vnto put my [Seale] (hand) the Daie & Yeare first aboue Written" in the document dated March 25, 1616.[4] So did his fellows in the theater: the clown Richard Tarlton sets his "hand and sealle with[t] the said penny therein fixed" in his will on September 3, 1588,[5] while Thomas Downton "Sealead with my seale & subscribred with my hand" his will on August 5, 1625.[6] Others gave away their signet rings as a part of their legacies. The actor Edward Alleyn gave "my seale ringe with my Armes to bee worne by the master and his succesors" in a will dated November 13, 1626;[7] the playwright James Shirley "likewise giue [my oldest son Mathias Shirley] my Cornelian seale ring" among other treasures in a will of July 1666.[8]

Leah might also have had her own signet ring; such rings go back to the period of the Torah (Exodus 35:22). Their stones were often engraved with the seven-branched candlestick, the menorah, and they were used by the Jewish women of the household, beginning in the Middle Ages, to light the Sabbath lamps. Most were carved by Jewish jewelers in Venice; they were not permitted as adornments for Jewish women in Poland until the reign of Sigismund Augustus (1506–1548) and then had to be inscribed with the words "Sabbation" or "Jerusalem," to remind Jews of the wrath of God and the punishment of sins.

Using such rings as a means of identification or authority as matters of cognition and recognition was not limited to wills; the drama of the time frequently employs them. Sir Giles Overreach gives his ring to "Sweet Master Allworth" in Philip Massinger's *A New Way to Pay Old Debts* (4.1.38–39; 4.3.113).[9] Sir Alexander gives his ring to Greenwit in *The Roaring Girl* of Thomas Middleton and Thomas Dekker; "He will believe this token" (5.2.82).[10] Juliet gives the Nurse her ring to authenticate her message to Romeo (*Romeo and Juliet*, 3.2.142–43; 3.3.163). York uses his to refortify the state treasury in Richard II's absence (2.2.92). Fenton uses his to court "sweet Nan" in *The Merry Wives of Windsor* (3.4.100). A disguised Kent uses his to send a messenger to French forces at Dover (*King Lear*, 3.1.46–47), specifying Cordelia in particular. Jachimo "By villany" gets Leonatus' ring (*Cymbeline* 5.5.142–43). Such rings are crucial stage properties and critical to resolutions and reconciliations in several of the comedies—*Two Gentlemen of Verona* (5.4), *The Merchant of Venice* (5.1), *All's Well That Ends Well* (5.3)—and the romances—*Pericles* (5.3.38) and *The Winter's Tale* (5.2.66). There are also other rings of office—John Shakespeare, the playwright's father, proudly wore an aldermanic ring of agate.

The ring that Jessica gives for a monkey, however, is unlikely to be the kind of merchants' signet that the usurer Shylock would use in driving home a financial arrangement. Rings were common in Shakespeare's day with both men and women, masters and servants, and easily obtained at fine mercers' shops as well as at county fairs, village fetes, and among pedlars' wares—John Heywood lists them along with "gloves, pins, combs, glasses unspotted, Pamades, hooks, and laces knotted" in "The Town P.P."[11] But Leah's ring to Shylock was something special, cognitively something that produces deep pathos. That he knows their relationship at the time—"I had it of Leah when I was a bachelor"—suggests that he is recalling her betrothal gift to him, a friendship ring given on a special occasion and for a special purpose. "That word [bachelor] shatters our image of this man Shylock" the actor Patrick Stewart commented when playing the role, "and we see the man that once was, a bachelor, with all the association of youth, innocence and love that is to come. Shakespeare doesn't need to write a pre-history of Shylock. Those two lines say it all."[12] As a token of love and commitment, a symbol of closure and eternity in its circular shape, the betrothal ring marked a particular relationship at a particular moment in time. His thoughts dwelling on Leah's ring may renew Shylock's sense of family begun with their courtship.

Such betrothal agreements knew only one outcome, the rite of holy matrimony. David Cressy writes that, "Though conducted in accordance with widely understood rules, courtship was no mere game, no idle dalliance. … To the middling sort and the elite, and perhaps through the lower ranks of respectable [Elizabethan] society, courtship was the acceptable pathway to marriage, a process of selection and bonding that secured a permanent union. By the time they reached their mid-twenties most young people were ready to embark on this perilous passage." [13] He further notes that, "Whether driven by love or scripted by social convention, courtship required the giving and acceptance of presents and tokens. Coins, rings, ribbons, gloves, girdles, and similar knick-knacks did the trick. Such gifts, usually passed by hand from the man to the woman, signaled the intimate strengthening of their bond. Their monetary value mattered less than their symbolism. Further gifts, most commonly a ring, changed hands when the couple was contracted, betrothed, or 'made sure'" (p. 263). An ecclesiastical lawyer of the time, Henry Swinburne, remarks that "love gifts and tokens. ... as bracelets, chains, jewels, and namely the ring" were "often used for the very arrabo or assured pledge of a perfect promise."[14] Elizabeth Yealand of Middleton-in-Teesdale reported to the Durham court in 1605 that she "was entreated by Agnes Newbie to go on an errand for her to James Handley, to signify her commendations verbally to him and to deliver him a ring of silver and a [root] of ginger, of which she had bit off a piece, willing [her] to tell him that for her sake it would content him to bite off another piece of the same ginger." He sent four apples in return; two French gold crowns, an enameled gold ring and a piece of Agnes' hair came back, convincing James of Agnes' seriousness.[15]

Figure 11: A betrothal ceremony from the monthly table for June in *The Holy Byble* (1579)

"That gifts were not simple items of value but potentially complex signifiers of promise and obligation," David Cressy tells us, is shown in the case of Joan Harris. She testified later in court that in 1623 Nicholas Harris

> brought a ring with him which he offered to leave with her as a gift from himself, and [Joan] divers times refused to receive any such thing of him. … After many denials made by her to take it, the said Nicholas vowing and protesting that he did not give it thereby to bind her in any way unto him, [she] at his great importunity or rather enforcement took it of him.

She tried several times to return the ring, Joan said, but "'Nicholas refused to take it again. And thereupon [she] conceiving it not fit for her to keep the said ring and not to give unto him something in recompense thereof sent unto him in like manner a ring of small price, which he received as she believeth'" (p. 265).

Such practices of gift giving—as, perhaps, in the case of Leah's gift to Shylock—concluded in contracts to marry. But such contracts could take many forms. Such a contract could be expressed most simply in the *verba de presenti*, speaking "I do" to bring about an immediate and indissoluble commitment, such as Mariana makes to Angelo in *Measure for Measure*. Such a contract could be a *verba de futuro*, a promise of a future union expressed by the words "I will." Separate vows revealed separate cognitive practices concerning rings. In his *Preparative to Marriage* (1591), Henry Smith witnesses a covenant based on words "spoken at a contract" at which he had been a kind of master of ceremonies. Daniel Rogers writes in *Matrimoniall Honovr: Or, The mvtuall Crowne and comfort of godly, loyall, and chaste Marriage* (1642) of "espousals, betrothings, assurings, contractings, affirmings (for they are all one) to be very solemn matters." "In some parts," adds Cressy, "the term was 'trothplighting,' which caught its essential feature of pledging. The word 'handfasting,' which called attention to the ritual action, was more commonly used in the north [of England]" (pp. 267–69). This particular ceremony, especially popular before the church courts of York and Durham from the 1570s to the 1620s, consisted of the holding and releasing of hands, the plighting of troths, kissing, drinking, and an exchange of betrothal rings. Such rituals were sometimes private, sometimes public. William Mead courted Margaret Rame of Great Waltham, Essex, for eighteen months before their betrothal in the house of Margaret's mother in 1577. The older woman was the only witness. She testified to a court that William took Margaret by the hand, saying, "I do here now take you to be my wife, and I do give you here my faith and troth; she the said Margaret holding him still by the hand answering, and here I do likewise give you my faith and troth, and do promise to be your wife." Having performed the traditional handfasting, the couple thought themselves "lawful man and wife before God," and made plans for a public church wedding. Only on the calling of the last of the three banns did Nicholas Satch rise to prevent the marriage by claiming a pre-contract. Such cases give point to Daniel Rogers' observation that a couple who made "private, mutual, free, unconditional promise" to each other to marry should nevertheless have "a more solemn and open binding expression of this former promise made, that it may be ratified and strengthened, as becometh a business of so great consequence." He urged a public ceremony conducted by someone of "gravity and experience," which would include prayers, acclamations, and thanksgivings of the witnesses to such a formal contracting as securing a firm foundation for matrimony.[16]

Christopher Marlowe's Jew Barabas in *The Jew of Malta* corrupts such private rituals by insisting that his daughter Abigail make love to Lodowick to arouse the jealousy of Mathias to the detriment of both men and for his own selfish joy. Barabas tells Abigail, "Daughter, a word more. Kiss him, speak him fair," and then aside to Abigail,

> And like a cunning Jew so cast about
> That you be both made sure ere you come out.

Barabas subsequently tells Abigail's preferred suitor Mathias that Ludowick has been courting his daughter.

Barabas: Pardon me though I weep; the governor's son
Will, whether I will or no, have Abigail.
He sends her letters, bracelets, jewels, rings.
Mathias: Does she receive them?
Barabas: She? No, Mathias, no, but sends them back.
And when he comes, she locks herself up fast;
Yet through the keyhole will he talk to her,
While she runs to the window, looking out
When you should come and hale him from the door.
Mathias: Oh, treacherous Lodowick!
Barabas: Even now as I came home, he slipped me in,
And I am sure he is with Abigail.
Mathias: I'll rouse him thence. [*He draws his sword.*] (2.3.237–72).[17]

Shakespeare's Jailer's Daughter, in *The Two Noble Kinsmen*, is sad rather than farcical, following from Shylock's own anguished sense of bereavement. According to the Wooer,

> Rings she made
> Of rushes that grew by, and to 'em spoke
> The prettiest posies—"Thus our true love's tied,"
> "This you may loose, not me." and many a one,
> And then she wept, and sung again, and sigh'd,
> And with the same breath smil'd, and kiss'd her hand.
> 2. *Friend* Alas, what pity it is! (4.1.88–94).

The rings of rush are especially poignant because, in the time of Shakespeare and the time of Shylock, the betrothal ring was very often the wedding ring as well.

For most members of Shakespeare's audience, however, the solemnization of marriage using the 1559 Prayer Book was prescribed by the 1559 Act of Uniformity, which "invoked sanctions as severe as life imprisonment for … refusal to use the prayer book or for denouncing it."[18] According to the Prayer Book, after the couple have pledged themselves,

> Then shall they again loose their hands, and the man shall give unto the woman a ring, laying the same upon the book, with the accustomed duty to the priest and clerk. And the priest taking the ring, shall deliver it unto the man to put it upon the fourth finger of the woman's left hand. And the man taught by the priest shall say: With this ring I thee wed, with my body I thee worship, and with all my worldly goods I thee endow. In the name of the Father, and of the Son, and of the Holy Ghost. Amen.
>
> Then the man leaving the ring upon the fourth finger of the woman's left hand, the minister shall say: Let us pray, O eternal God, creator and preserver of all mankind, giver of all spiritual grace, the author of everlasting life, send thy blessing upon those thy servants, this man and this woman, whom we bless in thy name, that as Isaac and Rebecca lived faithfully together, so these persons may surely perform and keep the vow and covenant betwixt them made (whereof this ring given and received is a token and pledge) and may ever remain in perfect love and peace together, and live according unto thy laws, through Jesus Christ Our Lord. Amen.

> Then shall the priest join their right hands together, and say: Those whom God hath joined together, let no man put asunder. Then shall the minister speak unto the people: Forasmuch as N. and N. have consented together in holy wedlock, and have witnessed the same before God and this company, and thereto have given and pledged their troth either to other, and have declared the same by giving and receiving of a ring, and by joining of hands, I pronounce that they be man and wife together. In the name of the Father, of the Son and of the Holy Ghost. Amen.[19]

The special placement of the ring was taken from old Latin missals that declared "a certain vein … runs from thence [the fourth finger] as far as the heart," and encouraged the later Tudor belief "that a particular vessel, nerve, vein or artery" connected the woman's ring finger directly to her heart. The physician Thomas Browne would later declare that the left hand was used rather than the right because that hand was generally less active and the ring less likely to be damaged.[20] This service was observed even in special circumstances, as in the instance of Thomas Filsby, a groom who was both deaf and dumb. Although the Book of Common Prayer prescribed marriage vows should be spoken, John Chippendale, Bishop of London, contrived a special marriage ceremony for Filsby and his bride, Ursula Bridget, in Leicester:

> First he embraced Ursula with his arms, took her by the hand and put the ring on her finger. Then he laid his right hand significantly upon his heart and after putting their palms together, he extended both his hands to heaven. Having thus sued for divine blessing, he declared his purpose to dwell with Ursula till death should separate them by closing his eyelids with his fingers, digging the earth with his feet as though he wished to make a hole in the ground and then moving his arms and body as if he were tolling a funeral bell. [21]

The central physical and cognitive act, unchanged, was the exchange of the marriage ring.

According to Cressy,

> Apologists for the ring went to some lengths to explain the antiquity, the propriety, and the symbolic benefits of its use in marriage. The view espoused in the fifteenth-century religious manual *Dives and Pauper*, that "the ring is round about and hath no end, in token that their love should be endless, and nothing

Figure 12: Frontispiece to Antoine de la Sale, *The Fyftene Joyes of Maryage* (1509)

depart them but death alone," found many echoes within the reformed Church of England. Richard Hooker endorsed the use of the ring on these grounds, as "an especial pledge of faith and fidelity, nothing more fit to serve as a token of our purposed endless continuance in that which we never ought to revoke." It signified "the perfect unity and indissoluble conjunction" of the married couple, "that their mutual love and hearty affection should roundly flow from one to the other," wrote the ecclesiastical lawyer Henry Swinburne, though he could not explain why only the women wore one.

The puritan Daniel Rogers, who may have been uneasy about the ritual exchange of the ring in marriage, nonetheless used the image of "the marriage ring ... beset with many rich jewels" to teach the virtues of honorable marriage; the jewels in the ring signified "humility ... peace ... purity ... [and] righteousness."

Another seventeenth-century writer similarly observed that "sober and knowing men have ever approved of the ring as the fittest and most significant pledge for the binding of that perpetual contract of reciprocal faith and affection that is between man and wife. (p. 342)

Matthew Griffith phrased it somewhat differently. "The husband," he writes, "presently puts the ring upon his wife's finger, that she may likewise understand, that her heart is shut up, and sealed from love, or thought in that kind, of any other man."[22] For the preacher Henry Smith, the first use of the ring was to represent the agreeable fit of husband and wife, "for if it be straighter than the finger it will pinch, and if it be wider than the finger it will fall off; but if it be fit, it neither pincheth nor slippeth."[23] Moreover, Cressy notes, for a great many writers, the ring "also served as a tag, a mark of ownership, and a visible advertisement of a woman's married state. The ring was a material symbol of the change from maidenhood to wifedom, and its transfer during the marriage service was, except for sedulous puritans, as crucial as the crown in coronation" (p. 343). In "The Bride," Samuel Rowlands claims that "with wedding rings, be wives of credit known."[24] "Some antiquarians," Cressy adds, "have also suggested that the ring represented an ancient bride price, given by the man to the woman as a symbol of purchase as well as a token of commitment. In folk belief, a wedding ring was empowered to conquer disease and to frustrate devils, and could be employed as part of the housewife's domestic medical armoury. Although, in protestant practice, they were no longer hallowed, this did not prevent people from treating wedding rings as if they were invested with sacred power" (p. 343). (By contrast, only men normally wore earrings, preferring a single earring as in the case of Sir Walter Raleigh or as we see in the Chandos portrait of Shakespeare. This custom was said to derive from the old sailor's habit of wearing one gold earring to cover the expense of his funeral if he died at sea or in a foreign land.)[25]

In 1567 Elizabeth Polsted's wedding ring cost 4s. with an added 9d. spent on extra gold, but rings could be simple or elaborate, with a considerable range in their price and value. Many were distinguished by individual private inscriptions or posies, revealing cognitive interpretations that individualized the more generally ceremonial rings. Grace Sherrington used the ring to become Lady Grace Mildmay with the inscription, "*Maneat inviolata fides.*" Thomas Whythorne, a court musician, commissioned a ring in 1569 with the inscription, "The eye doth find, the heart doth choose, and love doth bind till death doth loose." William Whiteway of Dorchester gave a wedding ring with the Latin words *Congugii firmi, et casti sum pigmis armoris* in 1620 although it is not certain he actually gave this ring during the service of solemnization.[26] "In the old catholic service, the priest sprinkled the ring with holy water and consecrated it with prayer; in the reformed English ceremony the act of laying the ring on the service book before putting it on to the woman's hand might still be interpreted as an act of hallowing," according to Cressy. "Reformers did not want to be told that this was simply the most convenient place to put it, but feared that it might be ignorantly interpreted as a sympathetic application of the book's sacred power. As late as 1590 in some parts of [heavily Catholic] Lancashire critics claimed that traditional clergy continued the catholic practice of 'transposing the ring from finger to finger at the several names of the father, the son, and the holy ghost,' and 'laying down and giving a large portion of money, as an endowment of the woman' in the course of the wedding ceremony" (p. 344).

B.J. Sokol and Mary Sokol observe that "the required giving of a ring or rings in the church ceremony, which was highly objectionable for Puritans, is also not seen in any Shakespearean setting in relation to solemnisation. The absence is all the more striking if we note that gifts of rings are frequently (but not inevitably) made either before, during, or after Shakespearian espousals" (p. 91) (as in *Two Gentlemen of Verona*, 2.2.4–6; *Richard III*, 1.2.189–212; *The Merchant of Venice*, 3.1.113; *Romeo and Juliet*, 3.2.142; *The Merry Wives of Windsor*, 3.4.99; *Twelfth Night*, 2.2.5; *Pericles*, scene xxii.61; and *Cymbeline*, 1.1.113). Sentimental poesies are satirized in *The Merchant of Venice* 5.1.147–50 and *Hamlet* 3.2.145. Those who elope, like Jessica, are especially endangered, as in the cases of Julia and Sylvia in *Two Gentlemen of Verona* and Helen in *Troilus and Cressida*.[27] The service in the Prayer Book is travestied in *Much Ado about Nothing* (4.1).[28] But wedding rings figure repeatedly in the drama of Shakespeare and his contemporaries, demonstrating the cognitive practices of a predominantly Protestant culture embedded in the drama of the time. Touchwood Junior orders a wedding ring from Yellowhammer in Thomas Middleton's *A Chaste Maid in Cheapside* (1.2). Guardiano plans the ceremony with a wedding ring for his foolish Ward in Middleton's *Women Beware Women* (3.4). Bracciano returns his wedding ring to Isabella in John Webster's *The White Devil* and she in turn refuses to give it to Francisco (2.1). The Second Pilgrim reports that the Cardinal has taken the Duchess' wedding ring in Webster's *The Duchess of Malfi* (3.4). And Shakespeare uses not one but two rings for the marriage of Sebastian and Olivia at the close of *Twelfth Night* (5.1.159). In 1810, the wife of a laborer in Stratford-upon-Avon working in a field neighboring the Holy Trinity churchyard found a gold ring, heavily encrusted, which was inscribed "W S" separated by a lover's knot.

Jewish wedding rings became popular in the sixteenth century. The bride's ring was placed on her middle finger by the groom, but it was not to be worn thereafter; rather, it was preserved by the family. Those traced to the Renaissance had a wide band with a model of a building with a cupola or high roof, said to represent a synagogue or the marital home, mounted on the bezel. Some buildings had pierced windows or even a movable weathervane. Hidden inside the bezel or inscribed on the band were the Hebrew letters for *Mazal Tov* (good luck) or the Hebrew initials for those words. Some rings depicted scenes or symbols from the Old Testament. Such rings were usually made of gold; in some cases, such as the ketubah, texts were housed within the ring.

Joan Evans has learned that the ring was then "the richest in association of all jewels: the Church sanctifies it in the marriage ring and the nun's ring; the Law recognizes it in the signet ring and the ring of investiture; sentiment ennobles it in the betrothal ring and the memorial ring; and the spell of magic touches it in the ring set with an amuletic stone [such as the turquoise] or engraved with a talismanic formula."[29] Rings were kept on a short wooden rod or on rolls of parchment. An inventory of the rings of Henry VIII compiled in 1527 reads: "Upon a finger stall seven rings, one a ruby, another an emerald, and a turquoise, another a table diamond, another a triangular diamond, another a rocky diamond."[30] His son Edward VI noted in his *Journal* for July 26, 1550, "Monsieur le Mareschal dined with me. After dinner saw the strength of the English Archers. After he had done, at his departure I gave him a Diamond from my finger, worth, by estimation, 150£, both for Pains, and also for my Memory."[31] His sister Mary Tudor was observed by the Venetian ambassador to be wearing two rings: "On her finger the Queen has two rings, with which she was espoused twice, first on her accession when she was crowned and confirmed the Treaty with France, and secondly when she became the wife of the present King of Spain."[32]

Evans goes on to note that "On all … rings characteristic inscriptions may be found: of all these inscriptions none bring us more closely into contact with the thoughts and feelings of their former wearers than the amatory inscriptions to be found on betrothal and marriage rings and other tokens exchanged between friends and lovers" (p. xi). In his *Arte of English Posie* in 1579, George Puttenham tells us epigrams "were called Nenia or Apophoreta, and never contained above one verse or two at ye moost, but the shorter the better. We call them

Figure 13: A fourteenth-century Jewish wedding ring with a pointed roof to symbolize the home and inscribed "Mazel Tov"

posies, and do paint them now-a-dayes upon the backsides of our trenchers of wood, or use them as devices in armes or in rings." The pithier, the better: "Deale trvly" or "Let Reson Rvle" or "This, with Mee." The will of Nicholas Fenay, a Yorkshire yeoman who died in 1617, left his son "my signet, or ringe of goulde, having these letters, N.F., for my name thereupon ingraven, with this notable posie about the same letters, viz Nosce teipsum, to the intente that my said son, William Fenay, in the often behouldinge and consideringe of that worthy poesye may be the better put in mynd of himselfe and of his estate, knowinge this, that to knowe a man's selfe is the beginninge of wisdom." In his *Remaines Concerning Britain* (1586), William Camden records posies found in rings of the period.

But commonplace books are the best source for such posies. The earliest and fullest is Harleian MS 6910 in the British Library; compiled shortly after 1596, it contains over 400 varied posies, such as "Neuer feare to loue" and "Nothing but to bee"; "Obey and commaund, yeeld and conquer" and "No hell to a dissembler" and, somewhat longer and more endearing, "I have don if you yeeld not soone; Pouertie preuenteth mee; Faint heart delayed too long." One posie in this manuscript—"If so I may, I will not say nay; I would if I might; I may not if I would; I may and will not"—is reminiscent of Hamlet's remark to Horatio before his final duel with Laertes: "If it be [now], 'tis not to come; if it be not to come, it will be now; if it be not now, yet it [will] come—the readiness is all" (5.2.220–22). But Hamlet is alert to such aphorisms; he says to Ophelia about the Prologue to "The Murder of Gonzago" that it too sounds like "the posy of a ring" (3.2.152). One of Robert Herrick's *Amatory Odes* is about just such a ring:

Julia, I bring to thee this ring,
Made for thy finger fit,
To shew by this that our love is,
Or should be, like to it.
Close though it be, the joint is free;
So when love's yoke is on
It must not fall nor fret at all
With hard oppression;
But it must play still either way,
And be too such a yoke
As not too wide to overslide,
Or be so strait to choke.
So we who bear this beam must rear
Ourselves to such a height
As that the stay of either may
Create the burthen light.
And as this round is nowhere found
To flow or else to sever,
So let our love as endless prove,
And pure as gold for ever.

A Helpe to Discourse (1640 edition) has twenty "posies for rings" as Jaques accuses Orlando of employing in *As You Like It* (3.2.270–72), while *The Card of Courtship* (1633) has "A double Poesie": "This hath no end, My sweetest friend. Our loues be so, No ending know."[33] So commonplace were posies in rings given as gifts that playgoers might be excused for imagining what personal private memento might have been inscribed in the ring which Leah once gave to her special bachelor.

Because it was also common for the betrothal ring to do double duty as the wedding ring, Leah's gift to Shylock may have been a betrothal ring, a wedding ring, or both. But it is clear it had a turquoise stone ("It was my turkis, I had it of Leah when I was a bachelor" [3.1.121–22]) that might harbor its own special cognitive significance. The turquoise was an especially popular stone for the time, often worn by men as gifts from women: Leah and Shylock practice a tradition not limited to Jews alone. George Steevens noted long ago that,

> A turquoise is a precious stone found in the veins of the mountains on the confines of Persia to the east, subject to the Tartars. As Shylock had been married long enough to have a daughter grown up, it is plain he did not value this turquoise on account of the money for which he might hope to sell it, but merely in respect of the imaginary virtues formerly ascribed to the stone. It was said of the Turkey-stone, that it faded or brightened in its colour as the health of the wearer increased or grew less.[34]

This means of communication from Leah to Shylock for his own well-being was another popular belief: Ben Jonson refers to it in *Sejanus* (1605) and Michael Drayton acknowledges it in *The Muses Elyziunm* (1630).[35] Philemond Holland's translation of *Pliny's Historie of the World* may have been a common source.[36]

Jackson Campbell Boswell has traced other, earlier significances attributed to the turquoise that may also have been in the minds of Shakespeare's playgoers:

> A great deal of folklore [had] become attached to the turquoise through the centuries. Turquoises were among the first stones to be collected and polished for ornamental purposes; they were found among the crown jewels of Queen Zer, wife of the second ruler of the second dynasty of Egypt, and there is evidence of mining operations in the first dynasty. Persian and Arabian mythology stresses the idea of fabulous wealth coming to him who dreams of the turquoise. The ancient Persians valued the stones highly and used them as charms to prevent horses from stumbling and their riders from falling off. The folklore surrounding the turquoise remained connected with horses when the stone became the talisman of the children of Naphtali. … In Europe throughout the Middle Ages and on into the

> Renaissance turquoise sentiment remained connected to horses, traveling, and fallings.[37]

In this last it shared attributes with the cramp ring: in *The Fyrst Boke of the Introduction of Knowledge* (1548), Andrew Borde notes that "Crampe rynges, the whyche rynges, worne on ones fynger, dothe help them the whyche hath the Crampe";[38] Thomas Middleton writes of a cramp ring with an agate stone in *The Roaring Girl* (1611; 4.2.23).[39]

But there are still other important cognitive possibilities. Where Shylock puts a monetary value on Jessica's theft of a German diamond—"A diamond gone, cost me two thousand ducats in Frankford!" (3.1.83–85)—the turquoise escapes such an appraisal, seems beyond financial reckoning of its worth. One reason Leah's gift means so very much to Shylock may come from other traditions. Boswell adds that "It was a Medieval conviction that certain stones became intimately familiar with the personality of their owners; that when the wearer of a turquoise fell ill the stone would change color out of sympathy, and if the owner came into the presence of disease, danger, or poison … the stone would warn him by changing color or otherwise manifesting alarm" (p. 482). In his *Secrete Wonders of Nature* (1569), Edward Fenton claims that "The Turkeys doth move when there is any perill prepared to him that weareth it."[40] The gift then would be a serious means by Leah to protect Shylock. So Thomas Nichols, sometimes of Jesus College, Cambridge, says in his *Lapidary* that the turquoise "is likewise said to take away all enmity, and to reconcile man and wife."[41] The very assurance of marital harmony between Shylock and Leah, then, between Jessica's father and mother, would rest on the significations of this stone. Leah, sums Boswell, "would have been familiar with the Eastern folklore of safety, prosperity, and love associated with the stone" (p. 483). Ironically, the stone was also known to bring about sterility in its owner. Clearly, this was not the case with Shylock—Leah gave birth to Jessica, after all—but Jessica may be acting on this very belief when she exchanges a ring with such powers for a pet identified with procreation. Shylock, too, may sense this if he sees her act signifying reproductivity in the company of the Christian Lorenzo: "Thou torturest me, Tubal" (3.1.120). The turquoise, then, can hold the power that assures Shylock of the double loss of his daughter and his family line.

Sir Thomas Cawerden, Master of the Tents for Elizabeth I and her first Master of the Revels, made out a will on August 24, 1559, in which he left to the "honorable Lord Clinton," later earl of Lincoln and Lord Admiral and a nobleman who had his own company of players from

1566, "a cup of £10 value as remembrance and testimony of his good will and to his wife a gold ring with a turquoise."[42] This ring was a mourning ring—a ring meant to memorialize the deceased on the hand of the recipient. That was shortly before Shakespeare's birth. Shortly after his death, on September 23, 1622, Robert Payne, possibly a patentee for the Children of the Queen's Revels from 1604 onwards, made Stephen Woodford and Ellis Crispe his overseers and left them "£3 each to buy rings. To brother Poole his ring which Mistress Skip gave him. To Mr. Andrew his ring with toad stone. To neighbour Plott 4 marks for ring."[43] On April 7, 1636, John Honyman, a boy actor with the King's Men, decided to "giue & bequeath to my loving ffather in law Iohn Sweetman twentie shillinges to buy him a ring withall," and continued, "Item I giue to euery one of my ffelowes the Players a ring of ten shillinges price." The fellow players included William Trigg, Alexander Gough, William Penn, Richard Baxter, Thomas Hobbes, William Hart, Richard Hawle, and William Patrick.[44]

Among the merchant class a funeral that William Lawrence attended in 1675 is representative. When he entered "the house of mourning" he saw that "The hall and parlour were hung with black cloth and escutcheons. There were about a hundred persons invited by tickets, and rings given,"[45] (Cognitively, these were the opposite of the rings convicted criminals gave at their deaths to their executioners.) A few years later, Ralph Verney recorded of Sir Richard Piggott's burial that "We that bore up the pall had rings, scarves, hat-bands, chamois gloves of the best fashion, and sarsenet escutcheons delivered to us; the rest of the gentry had rings, all the servants gloves."[46] David Cressy writes that "Claver Morris, a West-Country physician, spent almost £50 on his wife's funeral in 1689, and almost £12 more on her tombstone. [But] the greatest expense was on mourning gifts, £14.11s. on gloves and £8.15s. on rings" (p. 442). Rings were, he says, one of "the ingredients of a decent funeral" (p. 451), adding that "Urban patrician funerals in particular were renowned for their 'magnificent obsequies' with printed invitations, costly mourning gear, flambeau-lit processions, and distribution of gloves and rings" (p. 453). We find in the pawn accounts of Philip Henslowe, of the rival company, the Lord Admiral's Men, reference to "a gold ring with a death's head,"[47] a mourning ring doubtless similar to Berowne's reference in *Love's Labor's Lost* to "A death face in a ring" (5.2.612). The turquoise ring that the Shakespearean usurer Shylock has in mind when he cries out in anguish "Out upon her!" (3.1.120) of his daughter Jessica turns Leah's gift to him into his mourning ring for her in his mind's eye. In this he anticipates Jane Poley, the owner of the Boar's Head Inn, used as a playhouse, who in her will dated April 16, 1601, leaves "her best gold wedding ring" to her son John Pooley knight as a mourning ring.[48] Both would turn signs of wedding into signs of mourning, recording the double memorial of marital happiness and subsequent sorrow. For Shylock, such a transformation would barely rescue his sense of loss by changing it cognitively into an act of memorialization. But that ring alone must be exempt from the Frankfurt diamond and the "other precious, precious jewels" Jessica stole that he would put in her ear as she lies before him in the coffin of his mind's eye (3.1.83–90). Such a transformation, however, can also have the force of underscoring his sense of permanent loss.

In collecting the wills of those involved in the theater of Shakespeare's time, E.A.J. Honigmann and Susan Brock state how frequently mourning rings appear as bequests (p. 21). Sebastian Westcott, Master of Paul's, left "to Mystres Good wydowe, latelye the wief of doctour Good Physicion a ryng of gold with a blew stone, and to her dawghter Kynborowghe a ryng with three lemmowes small / To Mystres Sowthcote a gold ryng of some pretye fasshion to be made for her to the value of xl s/ To mr John Sowtchcotes wief the yonger a lyke ryng of gold of xl s price" (p. 51). The actor John Bentley bequeathed a gold ring to his mother (p. 56). Nicholas Brend, who owned the land on which the Globe was built, left "to Mr Doctor Lister and Mr Harlam 40s each to make them rings" (p. 68). Shakespeare's fellow actor Thomas Pope left to one friend a diamond ring, to another friend a gold ring with five opals, and to his housekeeper all the rest of his rings (p. 70). The playwright Edward Sharpham left a gold ring with a diamond in it (p. 78). The actor Thomas Greene was more specific: "I give to mr Gautres my baker tenn shillinges to be made a ringe as memoriall of me," he wrote, and then, "I give to mr Standley my brewer tenn shillinges to a memoriall ringe" (p. 91). The actor William Bird's widow required her sister to pay for such rings (p. 148). The actor Thomas Basse left many rings, including one to the actor Christopher Beeston. Mourning rings were also bequeathed by the playwright Arthur Wilson, the actor Ellis Worth, and the actor John Underwood: "I giue to my said Executors and Overseers for theire paines (which I intreat them to accept) the some of eleuen shillinges a peece to buy them rings to weare in remembrance of me" before leaving, in a later codicil, ten more seal rings, hoop rings, and mourning rings (p. 144). Nor was Shakespeare any different. He willed mourning rings to Hamnet Sadler, William Reynolds, Anthony Nash and his brother John as well as to the last three survivors of the Lord Chamberlain's/King's Men—Richard Burbage, John Heminges, and Henry Condell.[49] So commonplace was the bequest of mourning rings among actors, however, that the actor playing Shylock could have been wearing one himself through the performance of 1.2. The transformation could be made noticeable. An invisible property could be seen even when it was not announced, Leah's missing gift made awful in the realization of its absence. "I can make what merchandise I will. Go, Tubal, and meet me at our synagogue: go, good Tubal, at our synagogue, Tubal!" (3.1.128–30). It is at the synagogue that, for Shylock, wedding and funeral meet.

Leah is not the only woman who gives away a ring in *The Merchant of Venice*—Portia too gives a ring to Bassanio, just after he has chosen the right casket to obtain her hand in marriage and following her inventory of her wealth. But the ring-giving is redefined by Portia.

> now I was the lord
> Of this fair mansion, master of my servants,
> Queen o'er myself; and even now, but now,
> This house, these servants, and this same myself
> Are yours—my lord's!—I give them with this ring,
> Which when you part from, lose, or give away,
> Let it presage the ruin of your love,
> And be my vantage to exclaim on you (3.2.167–74).

The speech may mean to underscore the significance of the loss of Leah's ring in the adjoining plot in the scene immediately preceding this one, because otherwise the speech is an odd one, loading the gift with riches and making it conditional ("When you part from, lose, or give away, Let it presage the ruin of your love"). Rather than use this moment of handfasting to promise obedience, Portia reveals distrust. More than a gift, the ring is symbolic of her power and control which, following her own necessary obedience to her father's will, she now wishes to exercise. Bassanio's reply —

> But when this ring
> Parts from this finger, then parts life from hence;
> O then be bold to say Bassanio's dead (3.2.183-85)—

carries its own dreadful cognitive association with the parting of a ring and the parting (from Shylock's perspective) of Jessica's only meaningful life in the preceding scene. As for the present scene, it recalls Bassanio swearing his loyalty until death parts him from Portia; he subscribes, that is, to her test of loyalty by confirming the power of the ring to control his obedience, not as an occasion to offer it elsewhere.

Nor is Portia's willful testing here innocent; she may already have in mind her trick to disguise herself and go to Venice, perhaps to defend Antonio, but surely to assess his love and power for Bassanio and his for Antonio. This deliberate manipulation of the ring offered by the woman to the man makes a stark contrast to the ring Leah once gave to Shylock.

The final two scenes of *The Merchant of Venice*—4.2 and 5.1—build on another meaning of the ring altogether. It would seem to start in banter, a joke Portia and her maid Nerissa play on Bassanio and Gratiano while disguised as the lawyer Balthazar and his clerk:

Gratiano: My Lord Bassanio upon more advice
Hath sent you here this ring, and doth entreat
Your company at dinner.
Portia: That cannot be.
His ring I do accept most thankfully. …
Nerissa [Aside to Portia.]: I'll see if I can get my husband's ring,
Which I did make him swear to keep for ever.
Portia [Aside to Nerissa.]: Thou mayst, I warrant.
We shall have old swearing
That they did give the rings away to men (4.2.6–16).

In the final exchange here, an equivocation builds on the meaning of ring as both a loving and sexual gift. Portia seems especially interested in the possible pun of what Marjorie Garber calls "the symbolic or 'high' sense of a 'ring' … [and] the anatomical or 'low'" (50) in the following scene—"I gave my love a ring, and made him swear Never to part with it, and here he stands" (5.1.170–71)—followed by an excessive play on the word that could mean a band denoting eternal love or a woman's external sexual organ. This is the common reading of the play's final dialogue, but it takes on a more significant meaning when we realize Leah's gift to Shylock as the underlying subtext:

Bassanio: Sweet Portia,
If you did know to whom I gave the ring,
If you did know for whom I gave the ring,
And would conceive for what I gave the ring,
And how unwillingly I left the ring,
When nought would be accepted but the ring,
You would abate the strength of your displeasure.
Portia: If you had known the virtue of the ring,

Or half the worthiness that gave the ring,
Or your own honor to contain the ring,
You would not then have parted with the ring. …
I'll die for't but some woman had the ring! (5.1.192–208),

all the lines resonating with the giving away of Leah's ring, until plain-spoken Gratiano, who is forever aping and literalizing Bassanio, ends the play with an outright statement that calls on both the male and female anatomy: "Well, while I live I'll fear no other thing So sore, as keeping safe Nerissa's ring" (5.1.306-07). This is not the only time Shakespeare puns on the vulva or pudendeum (from the Latin gerundive of pudere, to be ashamed). Diana has this clearly in mind as she wards off Bertram in *All's Well That Ends Well*:

Mine honor's such a ring,
My chastity's the jewel of our house,
Bequeathed down from many ancestors,
Which were the greatest obloquy i' th' world
In me to lose. Thus your own proper wisdom
Brings in the champion Honor on my part,
Against your vain assault (4.2.45–51).

Jachimo has the same obscene meaning in mind when he tells Posthumus, in *Cymbeline*, that he will wager to win both Posthumus' ring to Imogen and Imogen herself: "She your jewel, this your jewel" (1.4.153). Thomas Middleton and William Rowley are employing the same pun when DeFlores emasculates Alonzo by cutting off his wedding ring, finger and all, in *The Changeling*:

Ha! what's that
Threw sparkles in my eye? Oh, 'tis a diamond
He wears upon his finger. It was well found,
This will approve the work. What, so fast on?
Nor part in death? I'll take a speed course then,
Finger and all shall off (3.2.20–25).[51]

So does John Fletcher in his send-up of Shakespeare's *Taming of the Shrew,* entitled *The Woman's Prize, or The Tamer Tamed*:

Sophonles: Pray, be not mistaken. By this light,
Your wife's as chaste and honest as a virgin,

For anything I know. 'Tis true she gave me
A ring.

Petruchio: For rutting (4.5.60–63).[51]

Such a frequent pun can normally seem stale, but not in *The Merchant of Venice*, where it is set in strong opposition to the powerfully positive, even reverent, meanings that can apply to Leah's ring as a personal signet, a betrothal ring, a wedding ring, an inscribed token, a gift to prevent illness and support marital harmony, a memorial or mourning ring. To Shylock, a ring in either sense of high or low measures his remembrance of things past. If so, we can see how Gratiano's apparently dissonant line can bring Shylock back into the play we thought he had left; and, in doing so, restore to him a stature that the trial scene in Venice so stoutly denied him. Leah's ring has much to tell us.

SHAKESPEARE'S BELLS

From nearly the start of his tragedy, Macbeth—King Duncan's "valiant cousin, worthy gentleman" (1.2.24)—desires the throne for himself. He responds quickly when meeting the three sisters on the heath, seeing in their comments hoped-for prophecies, "happy prologues To the imperial theme" (1.3.128–29). A short time later, his ambition is encouraged by his wife: "But screw your courage to the sticking place, And we'll not fail" (1.7.60–61). Yet, when the moment arrives to perform regicide, doubts overwhelm him. Sight supplies him with false visions; his mind's eye sees the immediate consequences. Dismissing his powers of sight, he is overcome by his sense of sounds—by his mind's ear—in what is perhaps the most ominous single speech of willed and unwilled cognition in the play:

> Is this a dagger which I see before me,
> The handle toward my hand? Come, let me clutch thee:
> I have thee not, and yet I see thee still.
> Art thou not, fatal vision, sensible
> To feeling as to sight? or art thou but
> A dagger of the mind, a false creation,
> Proceeding from the heat-oppressèd brain?
> I see thee yet, in form as palpable
> As this which now I draw.
> Thou marshal'st me the way that I was going,

And such an instrument I was to use.
Mine eyes are made the fools o' th' senses,
Or else worth all the rest. I see thee still,
And on thy blade and dudgeon gouts of blood,
Which was not so before. There's no such thing:
It is the bloody business which informs
Thus to mine eyes. Now o'er the one half world
Nature seems dead, and wicked dreams abuse
The curtain'd sleep; witchcraft celebrates
Pale Hecat's off'rings, and wither'd Murther,
Alarum'd by his sentinel, the wolf,
Whose howl's his watch, thus with his stealthy pace,
With Tarquin's ravishing [strides], towards his design
Moves like a ghost. Thou [sure] and firm-set earth,
Hear not my steps, which [way they] walk, for fear
The very stones prate of my whereabout,
And take the present horror from the time,
Which now suits with it. Whiles I threat, he lives:
Words to the heat of deeds too cold breath gives. [*A bell rings.*]
I go, and it is done; the bell invites me.
Hear it not, Duncan, for it is a knell,
That summons thee to heaven or to hell (2.1.33-64).

Even for Shakespeare, this soliloquy is remarkable. Macbeth's sudden—and self-acknowledged—hallucination finds its direct counterpart in the actual dagger now at his side, ready to hand, about to be drawn. He can realize, therefore, what is in his mind's eye. He can deny that vision and replace it with one that is "palpable." What is actual can then confirm what has only been imagined. By the end of the speech, though, Macbeth has surrendered vision, as at times unreliable, to sound, which may not be. In a transformation of cognition from hallucination to acknowledged sound, the actual sound—the stage direction that "A bell rings"—is overcome by a further hallucinated meaning giving it full and final agency: "the bell invites me." This bell—the stage property we do not see, but the shape of which we know so well—is compounded with a sound that calls even further attention to its absence.

Macbeth's mind darts about even as he would catch the nearest way. What that dagger would do—rather than Macbeth himself—is displaced by the celebration of Hecate and witchcraft: Macbeth, disdaining fortune, finds that she and her dark sisters are to blame. Then, present fears, rather than horrible imaginings, signal him to create

Figure 14: Bell ringers, reprinted from *Samuel Pepys' Penny Merriments*

"wither'd Murther," a calculated embodiment who will perform the desired act as Macbeth's willed substitute as if, in the dark recesses of Macbeth's brain, Murder has become an impersonal and independent force. Horrible imaginings, in turn, take over present fears, and Macbeth likens his stealthy advance on the King to Tarquin's approach to Lucrece, a movement, in Macbeth's turbulent anxiety, caused by Duncan's attraction, so that ravishment of the King is motivated by the overpowering seduction on Duncan's part. Blame belongs to the victim, not the perpetrator. What finally resolves such impossible mental turmoil is not perceived illusions or conceived delusions, but a single sound: "the bell invites me." "With the tolling of the bell," John Turner writes, Macbeth "abandons language altogether. 'I go, and it is done': a final prolepsis, containing the deed within the intention, and then the lifelong discovery that something which is done is not necessarily over."[1]

In a play that continually opens its scenes with questions—"When shall we three meet again?" (1.1.1); "What bloody man is that?" (1.2.1); "Where hast thou been, sister?" (1.3.1); "Is execution done on Cawdor?" (1.5.1)—and with riddling binaries—fair is foul and foul is fair; when a battle is lost and won; when whatever is is not—what bell is it that Macbeth hears so decisively? What works for Macbeth with such cognitive force and assurance? It could be the bell that commonly rang the curfew—"Well, tis 9. a clock, tis time to ring curfew," the Sexton remarks in *The Merry Devil of Edmonton*, a play attributed to the King's Men, "his Maiesties Seruants, at the Globe, on the bank-side" in 1608.[2] A great bell tolled dusk in Stratford-on-Avon throughout Shakespeare's life. Or it might be the night bell that summons a ghost such as that of Tarquin, as it seems to summon the Ghost of Hamlet, according to both Bernardo and Marcellus (*Hamlet*, 1.1.39–40). Most critics, however, have considered it to be not a sound in Macbeth's ear but rather an actual agent in the play, the collusive act of Lady Macbeth. For, just before his soliloquy, Macbeth has ordered an unnamed servant to "Go bid thy mistress, when my drink is ready, She strike upon the bell" (2.1.31–32) and his o'ervaulting ambition has subtly but decisively changed the command *to* Lady Macbeth to one *from* her, her signal to him for a bedtime drink converted to a call for regicidal action. It may be, of course, that this man of extraordinary imagination—who can see past and future in an instant, daggers where there apparently are none—is also deluded once again, hearing a bell that does not yet ring. He wills the bell and its command into being instead, just as he wills the dagger, both enabling the three sisters' observations into historic truths, premise into performance, a "supernatural soliciting" (1.2.130) that he envisions into a deed of untrammeled consequences.

The First Folio provides the direction, though, and it most likely refers to the small hand-held bell that was a stage property frequently used to signal events. Alexander uses such a bell to call Bernardo several times in *The Devil's Charter* by Barnabe Barnes (1606; sigs. B3, E3, G1, G2). A vintner employs one to call his drawers in Alexander Brome's *The Weeding of Covent Garden* (1632; 33). One is even seen but not heard in William Davenant's *News from Plymouth* (1635): "A curtain drawn by Dash (his clerk) Trifle discovered in his study. Papers, taper, seal and wax before him, bell" (167).[3] What seems clear, however, is that Macbeth has transformed the handbell as an invitation to drink to induce sleep into an invitation to kill, to make sleep permanent. Then, his fears that the world is watching and that the sound of the very stones will betray him, suggest he is cognitively transforming the bell into more than an invitation; when his action is discovered, this could become an alarm bell such as the one struck in *Othello* (2.3.160) during the fight that Iago stages between Cassio and Roderigo. "Who's that which rings the bell?" asks Iago; "Diablo, ho! The town will rise" (*Othello*, 2.3.161–62). "A bell tolls; a confused cry within" (4.3.s.d.) is just such a bell when we learn of the supposed death of Quomodo in Thomas Middleton's *Michaelmas Term* (1606); the bell that DeFlores sets off in *The Changeling* by Thomas Middleton and William Rowley

(1602; 5.1.73) is another.[4] In still a third transformation, Macbeth is a fatal bellman: "Hear it not, Duncan," he says, adopting this role, "for it is a knell, That summons thee to heaven or to hell." He is now the night watchman, who cried the hours by ringing a bell in Shakespeare's England; and he is also the bellman who was the last to visit a condemned person before his death, as in John Webster's *The Duchess of Malfi* (1614; 4.2.173–75), suggesting Macbeth is determined to see Duncan as one already condemned before the regicide, perhaps by the sisters, perhaps by the conspiracy between him and his wife, perhaps by Duncan's actions, perhaps by his own disciplined will. Macbeth's active imagination invited playgoers to recognize possibilities, multiple significances, bells could have in their culture. At each stage, so fair and foul a night Macbeth had not before seen, even in his mind's eye, nor heard in his mind's ear. The sound of a bell, interrupting and destroying the silence Macbeth seeks, commands attention and demands a response, from Macbeth, from us, that can accommodate its noise and can explain it if not finally explain it away.

The silence that Macbeth relies on is what calls particular attention to the bell. The knocking at the gate that will follow (2.3.0 s.d.)—the Porter will use the word *knock* eleven times—suggests *Macbeth* is a play peculiarly susceptible to noises. But Shakespeare's stage could be as full of noises as Caliban's island. Peter Ackroyd notes their frequency. The players "simulated the sound of horses' hooves and of bird-song, of bells and cannons. Voices off-stage amplified battle scenes with cries of 'kill, kill, kill,' loud shouts, shrieks, and general clamour. There were fireworks available, for lightning. … When the directions called for 'thunder' a sheet of metal was shaken vigorously. … The sound of pebbles in a drum could counterfeit the sea, and a piece of canvas tied to a wheel could mimic the wind. The sound of dried peas upon a metal sheet would substitute for rain."[5] In their *Dictionary of Stage Directions in English Drama, 1580–1642*, Alan C. Dessen and Leslie Thomson note several kinds of bells used by Shakespeare's company: "(1) a tower bell that sounds an alarm, announces a death, or gives the time, (2) a door or gate bell [that announces someone has just arrived], (3) a handbell used to call servants" (p. 28); at this point in *Macbeth*, all three bells might seem to converge. Such bells were staples for the players. Philip Henslowe's inventory of stage properties used by the Admiral's Men at the time lists several of them: Bruce R. Smith has noted "'ii stepbells, & j chyme of belles, 6 j beacon' [which] has been interpreted by Michael Hattaway as sets of various kinds of bells: clock bells ('steeples'), and a bell for ringing alarums ('a beacon')."[6] Each of these bells nevertheless had a particular purpose; as with Macbeth's bell, they denoted a special moment in time, just as they did in Shakespeare's culture. "The clock hath strucken twelve upon the bell," Dromio of Ephesus tells us in *The Comedy of Errors* (1.2.45), while later on Dromio of Syracuse remarks, "the bell, 'tis time that I were gone; It was two ere I left him, and now the clock strikes one," causing Adriana to reply, "The hours come back! that did I never [hear]" (4.2.53–55). "The Windsor bell that strook twelve," says Falstaff in *The Merry Wives of Windsor* when he appears as Herne the Hunter (5.5.1). A bell called the boy Shakespeare to the King Edward VI Grammar School each morning and called him back at one o'clock after the dinner recess. A bell closed the market in Shakespeare's Stratford-upon-Avon at 11 a.m. as it closes the market in Thomas Middleton and Thomas Dekker's *The Roaring Girl*—"Hark the bell rings, come gentlemen," says Goshawk; "where shall's all munch?" (1611; 2.1.418–19).[7] A bell opens the market in *l Henry VI*—"Enter, go in, the market bell is rung" (3.1.16). Bells followed Shakespeare to London; the Shoreditch High Street was known for its peal of bells. Such bells measured daily life, recorded it, as one seems to accompany Macbeth's passage from hastily talking with Banquo to moving toward the sleeping Duncan measures his, if in a special way.

But bells could be special even when less personal. "Special days called for special actions" David Cressy sums. "The major holidays, anniversaries, and successes of Tudor and Stuart England were marked by festive activities in the streets and villages as well as by events at court and notations in the calendar. People of the sixteenth and seventeenth centuries could draw on a versatile vocabulary of celebration," and they did so by "ringing bells, shooting guns, sounding instruments, or raising cheers."[8] The nobleman Toclio remarks that bells proclaim just such an occasion: "Oh, my Lord," he says to Cador, the earl of Cornwall, "the Court's all fill'd with rumor, the City with news, and the Country with wonder, and all the bells i' th' Kingdom must proclaim it, we have a new Holyday a coming" in *The Birth of Merlin*, a play that, according to the title page of the 1662 text, was "Written by William Shakespear, and William Rowley."[9] A bell could proclaim the change of rule. Conversely, late scenes in Thomas Dekker's *Shoemakers' Holiday* repeatedly emphasize the pancake bell of Shrove Tuesday instituted by Simon Eyre:

> I have procured that upon every Shrove Tuesday, at the sound of the pancake bell, my fine dapper Assyrian lads shall clap up their shop windows and away. This is the day, and this day they shall do't. Boys, that day are you free. Let masters care, and prentices pray for Simon Eyre (1599; xvii.60–67).[10]

To the playgoers at the Globe, long accustomed to bells voicing special occasions, the ringing bell that finally sends Macbeth on his way, the dagger that had been conventional for the Vice of earlier morality plays in his hand, could have seemed momentous, perhaps recalling the unexpected freedom given on Shrove Tuesday, itself a seismic political shift.

Yet such customary bells alongside such very special bells were usually drowned out by the constant pealing of church bells. Feste jokes about the triple church bells announcing services at St. Benet's church in *Twelfth Night* (5.1.37–40). The joke depends on a keen awareness by playgoers of Elizabethan and Jacobean London as an "acoustically dense soundscape," Bruce Smith notes. "Loudest of all, apparently, was the bell of St. Mary-le-Bow. John Stow, who in his Survey of London pronounces the church 'more famous then any other Parish Church of the whole Cittie, or suburbs,' notes how the bell's ringing signalled rhythms of the workday. Any lateness would prompt apprentices to complain, 'Clarke of the Bow bell with the yellow lockes, / For thy late ringing thy head shall haue knockes'" (p. 53).[11] In *Parimedes*, Robert Greene emphasizes that church bell when he writes of Tamburlaine's ranting that "everie word [filled his] mouth like the faburden of Bo-Bell" (p. 8). Of parish bells generally, David Cressy tells us that "None could escape their clamour. Often the bells could be heard at a distance of a mile or more, ringing above the routine noises of urban or village life. … In the middle of the sixteenth century, the preacher Hugh Latimer noted that 'if all the bells in England should be rung together at a certain hour, I think there would be almost no place but some bells in England might be heard there.'" According to Cressy,

> Bells were rung regularly to summon worshippers to service. Traditionally they rang at weddings and funerals (joyous peals at the one, mournful knells [like the one Macbeth hears in his mind's ear] at the other), marking individual rites of passage. They sang out too at midsummer and new year, and on the major Christian holy days. At the parish of St. John, Ousebridge, York, for example, the ringers rang through the night on Christmas Eve 1601 "untill the middle bell-string broke next morning." When the seventeenth century created a new calendar of secular, dynastic and patriotic anniversaries which overlaid the traditional cycle of the Christian year, the bells marked it accordingly. … Most of the ten thousand or so parish churches had bells which were rung on festive and ceremonial occasion. Some were simple arrangements with one or two bells,

> others were finely tuned peals of six or eight designed to make a joyful noise. Most bells were sources of local pride which made inroads into parish funds. … Churchwardens' records are dotted with expenditures on beer and cheese for the bellringers, and payments for hanging, oiling, framing, setting, and repairing the bells (pp. 69–70).

Such sounds the doctor Helkiah Crooke finds harmful in his *Microcosmographia: A Description of the Body of Man* in 1615: "we see often times that the noyse of great Ordinance or of Bels, if a man be in the steeple, yea an intollerable cold ayer doe affect the Eare with paine and dolour; somtimes also breake the Tympane from whence deafnesse followeth." [12] Little wonder that Clerimont finds Morose so overcome by "the perpetuity of ringing bells" that he "has made him … a room with double walls, and treble ceilings, the windows close shut and caulked; and there he lives by candlelight" in Ben Jonson's *Epicoene, or the Silent Woman* (1609; 1.1.200–04). [13] Cognitively, bells were both highly symbolic and commonplace, as if Macbeth's bell could be understood simultaneously in both ways.

But bells might have other associations for Shakespeare's playgoers—they were connected to Puritans, for instance. In the 1630s, in London, Puritans rang bells for an entire hour before the service at six in the morning in Budget Row so as to encourage as many men and women as possible to attend. At the same time, though, they harbored a fierce distaste for bells associated with impure pagan or papist practices of an earlier age, such as the churchbells that had marked the Roman services of matins and evensong. There was also the despised practice of the Roman church's sacring bell, rung to request parishioners to put aside their own prayerbooks during the celebration of the Catholic Mass in order to acknowledge and witness the moment of consecration when the priest elevated the Host and, subsequently, the chalice. According to Eamon Duffy in *The Stripping of the Altars*, "The sacring at the Sunday Mass would certainly have been especially solemn, surrounded by torches and accompanied by the mutter of elevation prayers from one's fellow parishioners, and the tolling of one of the great bells, so that those abroad would know, kneel, and share."[14] The sacring bell, along with the Mass, had been forbidden by the church injunctions in Elizabeth's reign, but the practice had not entirely faded from the memory of Shakespeare's audiences in a latter-day, officially Protestant England. In *The Merry Devill of Edmonton,* the Prioress of Cheston tells Millisent, echoing Macbeth's appropriation of the word *knell* while redefining the sound as a sign of life rather than death,

You shall ring the sacring bell,
Keepe your howers, and tell your knell,
Rise at midnight to your mattens,
Read your Psalter, sing your lattins.
And when your blood shall kindle pleasure,
Scourge your selfe in plenteous measure (3.1.42–47).

Thinking of bells they knew, playgoers could cognitively associate the sacring bell—announcing a sacred act by someone spiritually ordained—with Macbeth's demonic act. Surely Macbeth's blood is kindled by the bell he hears; surely he sees himself as an agent scouring the state for the three sisters rather than for God. In Shakespeare and John Fletcher's *Henry VIII, or All Is True* for the same company that staged *The Merry Devill of Edmonton*, the earl of Surrey threatens to startle Wolsey "Worse than the sacring bell" (3.2.295). Playgoers at *Macbeth* could also be startled, but, for Macbeth, the bell sanctions his deed and reinforces his actions, lifting a knife—instead of a Host—to the sound of the bell.

Yet Macbeth is not alone in imposing on the sound of a bell his own personal significance, nor are the playgoers attending his actions. The plays of the time offer numerous instances that would lead playgoers to sense the personal meaning that could set a bell marvelously and memorably apart. King John uses a midnight bell to calm Hubert, for example:

If the midnight bell
Did with his iron tongue and brazen mouth
Sound on into the drowsy race of night;
If this same were a churchyard where we stand,
And thou possessed with a thousand wrongs;
Or if that surly spirit, melancholy,
Had bak'd thy blood, and make it heavy, thick, …
Then, in despite of brooded watchful day,
I would into thy bosom pour my thoughts.
But, ah, I will not! yet I love thee well,
And by my troth I think thou lov'st me well (*King John*, 3.3.37–55).

And when Antony uses a similar tactic in *Antony and Cleopatra*—

Call to me
All my sad captains, fill our bowls once more;
Let's mock the midnight bell (4.1.182–84)

— we can sense the false joviality, his celebration on his success on the second day of battle and his anxiety for the third. Both King John and Antony may harness the midnight bell to their own special needs and purposes, as Macbeth harnesses the handbell that he hears to his.

It was not at all uncommon in early modern England to assign a personal sense of security to the ringing of bells. "Besides signalling events to the listening community," David Cressy tells us, "bells were thought to have protective qualities. Medieval bells were holy, and were baptized or sacralized before being hung. They were believed to have a mystic potency, an ability to cleanse the air and to drive away devils. In early modern England it was still a popular belief that the spirit world could be intimidated through noise. The passing bell was said to deter demons hovering about a person who was dying. Bells were likewise employed during thunderstorms to drive away the evil spirits that were thought to be clashing in the air" (p. 70). Shakespeare makes a point of this too. In hearing the bell, Macbeth may even sense the security of his wife's partnership; "What cannot you and I perform upon Th' unguarded Duncan?" Lady Macbeth has told him.

The bell in *Macbeth* can underscore yet another meaning, convey another signal, to the playgoers at the Globe: it can indicate a change in kingship; in Macbeth's mind as in the playgoers' minds, it can announce a new succession to the rule. The loud peals of bells that announced Crownation Day in Elizabethan England "was the first annual concert of bells that was not tied to the Christian year," Cressy observes (pp. 50–51). In some areas of England, Accession Day on November 17 successfully built on the earlier festivities perpetuating the memory of St. Hugh of Lincoln, initially strengthening that tradition, but, by 1567, it was surely and uniquely the Queen's day when the bells rang in Lambeth. "The churchwardens of the City parish of St. Botolph without Bishopsgate paid one shilling 'to the ringers that rung for the queen's majesty's entrance of the eleventh year of her grace reign, which was the 17th day of November 1568,'" Cressy writes. "St Peter Cheap rang in 1568, and other parishes followed suit. The practice was widely adopted in southern England in 1570 or soon after, and spread during the following years to parishes throughout the country. The university towns of Oxford and Cambridge were quick to ring for the queen, but the accession day custom spread more slowly in the north. Yorkshire parishes were 'ringing for the queen's majesty's reign' by the mid-1570's" (p. 52). In 1574, churchwardens at Mere, Wiltshire, recorded spending 2s.4d. for ringers as well as for meat, drink, and candles. In 1580, the vestry at St. Mary Adlermanbury voted 6s.8d. for annual expenses commemorating the Queen's Crownation Day;

at St. Edmund's, Salisbury, bellringers were given 4d. or 6d. to ring bells at Christmas, Easter, Ascension Day, and Whitsunday but they received 8s. on Crownation Day in 1587. That year churchwardens paid John Brewer to work for three days mending the bells against Crownation Day in Swaffham, Norfolk. Maidstone, Ipswich, Coventry, and Nottingham staged plays and pageants in their streets. Other towns feasted. In the village of Tilney, Norfolk, the churchwardens spent 3s. on "a kilderkin of beer upon the day of coronation" in 1583. The city of Norwich fired ordnance and put on torch-lit processions attended by waits and trumpeters. At Cambridge, the university added Crownation Day to those occasions when doctors were required to wear their scarlet gowns. A popular verse assigned to the 1580s goes like this:

> Adore November's sacred sev'nteenth day,
> Wherein our second sun began her shine.
> Ring out loud sounding bells; on organs play;
> To music's mirth let all estates incline;
> Sound drums and trumpets, renting air and ground.
> Stringed instruments strike with melodious sound.

But such an occasion could be parodied. James Shapiro notes that the

> students at Lincoln College, Oxford—which had strong Catholic leanings—would annually on November 17 commemorate their patron saint, Saint Hugh of Lincoln. Sometime around 1580, Oxford's mayor caught them in the act of ringing bells at All Hallow Church, and accused them of doing so in memory of the passing of [the Catholic] Queen Mary [Elizabeth's half-sister and predecessor]. The quick-witted students avoided punishment by claiming that they were simply ringing bells in honor of Elizabeth's accession. The chastened mayor … then ordered the rest of Oxford's churches to ring their bells. Historians have noted that in some parts of England where payments were made for bell ringing on this day, accounts sometimes specify that they are to honor Elizabeth and sometimes Saint Hugh. If the authorities were unsure for whom the bells tolled, how could those toiling in the fields that day know with any certainty who was being honored: Saint Hugh? Mary? Elizabeth?[15]

By 1600, fresh oil, rope, leather, and woodwork were needed for the bells of Holy Trinity Church in Cambridge. In addition to bells on November 17, 1602, the lectern at St. Stephen Coleman Street was ablaze with six pounds of candles.[16] All these bells champion and commemorate an ascension to the throne. Shakespeare's Henry IV can hear bells when he imagines his son Prince Hal crowned before him in his anguished reprimand:

> What, canst thou not forbear me half an hour?
> Then get thee gone, and dig my grave thyself,
> And bid the merry bells ring in thine ear
> That thou art crowned, not that I am dead (4.5.109–12).

Henry IV and Macbeth share their own menu of cognitive associations in linking bells, crowns, and usurpation.

Bell-ringing also proclaimed Elizabeth's arrival as she made her progresses about the English countryside, underscoring the use of bells to announce rulers. To make certain this would be the case, instructions were given to city churches well before her arrival. In June 1563, the Queen went by water from Whitehall to Greenwich to the sound of bells rung at the riverside parishes. Indeed, those who failed to follow the instructions were fined 6s.8d. Similarly, churchwardens of Great St. Mary's, Cambridge, paid a fine of 2s.2d. when the Queen's almoner's servant failed to ring the bell to announce her coming in 1566. If such local authorities neglected to do their duty, church doors could be nailed shut until they paid their fines. Few parishes failed to obey the royal commands.[17] Nor did the use of bells to proclaim and then annually celebrate the sovereign die with Elizabeth I. When James IV of Scotland and I of England succeeded to the throne on March 24, 1603, bells proclaimed the transfer of rule over all of England as they did once again on St. James's Day when he was finally crowned. He personally dismantled Elizabeth's celebrations, moving the royal anniversary from November 17 to the springtime. Parishes purchased prayer books proper for the new celebration on March 24. But James inaugurated other days of royal celebration as well. Bells marked attempted usurpations and regicide as in *Macbeth*. Bells rang out each August 5 to recall his escape from the Gowrie conspiracy in Perth, Scotland, when a group of rebellious nobility attempted to capture and kill him before he miraculously escaped—or so the story went. And each November 5 bells were rung again to commemorate the exposure of the Gunpowder Plot in which a group of disaffected Catholics were said to have laid plans to blow up the royal family as well as all of the state and church leaders by placing barrels of gunpowder underneath Parliament House to be set off at the opening of Parliament in 1605.

The bell that passes the crown can do so only upon the change of sovereign. Macbeth is staunchly aware of this: the bell that invites him is for Duncan "a knell, That summons thee to heaven or to hell" (2.1.63–64). Thomas More is also aware of what came to be called the passing bell in a play named for him: "The bell (earth's thunder) soon shall toll my knell," he tells Lady Alice (1595; 4.4.143).[18] About the same time, in *Venus and Adonis*, Shakespeare was describing a doomed rabbit in much the same traditional way: "And now his grief may be compared well To one sore sick that hears the passing bell" (701–02). As for the rabbit, this was the bell that was especially feared. According to Cressy, "Parish bells tolled when a person was dying, then signaled that someone was dead, and often rang again at the time of their burial" as it did in 1579 for Shakespeare's eight-year-old sister Anne: according to the Stratford parish records, "the bell & paull for Mr Shaxpers dawghter." "Sometimes the bells sounded for hours on end, ringing both day and night," Cressy continues in *Birth, Marriage, and Death*. "Their purpose was to show respect, to alert the community, to summon attendants to the bedside or the graveside, to bring comfort to the living and the dying, and to assist the parting person by prompting neighbours to their prayers."[19] Some even hoped it would aid the shrouded corpse by sanctifying the soul as it left the body in its winding-sheet. This last belief, however, was tainted as peculiarly Catholic by many, and Edward VI's commissioners sent out orders to the parishes to "abstain from such unmeasurable ringing for dead persons at their burials," and to ring one bell only "at such time as sick persons lieth in extreme danger of death," and, later, to ring "moderately" at funerals.[20]

The official state "Advertisements" ordered the church bell to be tolled "when any Christian body is passing … and after the time of passing, to ring no more but one short peal, and one before the burial, and another short peal after the burial."[21] In 1571, Edmund Grindal, archbishop of York, sanctioned the tolling of the passing bell in his archdiocese "to move people to pray for the sick person," but he objected to ringing a bell after someone had died. Rather, he ordered "one short peal" as sufficient for funerals; anything more, he said, would be "superfluous or superstitious."[22] The Jacobean bishop William Chaderton of Lincoln made the passing bell an object of parish visitations. You must, he directed, ask "whether doth your clerk or sexton, when any is passing out of this life, neglect to toll a bell, having notice thereof; or the party being dead, doth he suffer any more ringing than one short peal, and before his burial one, and after the same, another."[23] His point, as with so many others, was not to eliminate the passing bell such as the one Macbeth may imagine he hears, but rather to reduce the funeral knell to moderate the bell's use and to avoid recalling old Catholic beliefs and superstitions. What ringing there was should be focused on the moment of dying—the funeral bell that the poet John Donne warns may ring for any man. This Donne thought to be useful, because, he said, "it brings the congregation together and unites God and his people."[24] The Jacobean preacher Thomas Adams, from Bedfordshire, remarked,

> It is a custom not unworthy of approbation, when a languishing Christian draws near to his end, to toll a heavy bell for him. Set aside the prejudice of superstition and the ridiculous conceits of some old wives, whose wits are more decrepit than their bodies, and I see not why reasons may not be given to prove it, though not a necessary, yet an allowed ceremony.

Moreover, one of the virtues of the passing bell was that "it puts into the sick man a sense of mortality. … Thus with a kind of Divinity, it gives him the ghostly counsel to remit the care of his carcase, and to admit the cure of his conscience." The very sound of the bell

> excites the hearers to pray for the sick . … The bell, like a speedy messenger, runs from house to house, from ear to ear, on thy soul's errand, and begs the assistance of their prayers. … As the bell hath often rung thee into the temple on earth, so now it rings thee unto the church in heaven, from the militant to the triumphant place.[25]

Playgoers cognitively accustomed to such a tradition could confirm the anticipated death of Duncan in the ringing of a bell.

Still, there was a good deal of variation among the parishes, often dependent on their equipment, their status, and the money available to pay the bell-ringers. It was reported in 1562 in Hollingbourne, Kent, that "they use three peals in ringing at burials," excessive but not illegal. In 1575 at Kettlewell, Yorkshire, Grindal was upset to learn that "the bell is not tolled to move the people to pray for the sick" when death was near. Lancashire was said to have "excessive ringing for the dead. … But while the party lieth sick, they will never require to have the bell knolled, no, not at the point of death."[26] In 1619 in Cropredy, Oxfordshire, churchwardens reported that "the bell is usually for the most part tolled when they are passing out of this life while in neighboring Holton in 1631 bell-ringers "rang two or three peals for Mrs.

Horseman," who had been excommunicated, and then celebrated with "a bottle of drink and a little loaf of bread brought them to the church" by Mrs. Horseman's maid.[27] William Reade, a minister in Cropredy, conversely denied ringing the passing bell for Margery Winter and in 1633 Ambrose Robinson of Long Preston, Yorkshire, for some unrecorded reason, put "sand and gravel into the bell stocks while certain of the parish were ringing for the burial of a corpse."[28] At Wells Cathedral in 1612, the sound of the bells was restricted by limiting their duration to half an hour.[29]

Indeed, "parishes spend much money in harmoniously-sounding bells," Philip Julius, duke of Stettin-Pomerania, writes in 1602, "that one being preferred which has the best bells. The old queen is said to have been pleased very much by this exercise, considering it as a sign of the health of the people. They do not ring the bells for the dead, but when a person lies in agony, the bells of the parish he belongs to are touched with the clappers until he either dies or recovers again."[30] It is another way the brain could register the pain and anticipated arrival of a death that will affect the wealthy and the impecunious alike. Vindice notes how, in the anonymous *Revenger's Tragedy*, "a great rich man lies adying, and a poor cobbler tolls the bell for him" (1606; 4.2.71).[31] Shakespeare's Lord Capulet bemoans the death that cuts short the marriage of Juliet: "All things that we ordained festival Turn from their office to black funeral: Our instruments to melancholy bells, Our wedding cheer to a sad burial feast" (*Romeo and Juliet*, 4.5.84–87), while at the tomb, his wife takes the unexpected death as a personal sign: "O me, this sight of death is as a bell That warns my old age to a sepulcre" (5.3.206-07). Both are cognizant of the passing bell. At her maimed rites, Ophelia's right to the passing bell is questioned by the Doctor over the subsequent protests of Laertes: "Her death was doubtful," he comments,

> And but that great command o'ersways the order,
> She should in ground unsanctified been lodg'd
> Till the last trumpet; for charitable prayers,
> [Shards,] flints, and pebbles should be thrown on her.
> Yet here she is allow'd her virgin crants [garland],
> Her maiden strewments, and the bringing home
> Of bells and burial (*Hamlet*, 5.1.227–34).

The most bitter recognition of the passing bell comes from Christopher Marlowe's Barabas, who says at the opening of Act 4 of *The Jew of Malta*, "There is no music to a Christian knell."[32] The stark denial of a passing bell—"no mournful bell shall ring her burial"—is the most damning punishment Lucius can devise for Tamora (*Titus Andronicus* 5.3.197).

As the burial bell rang, the coffin was carried to the parish church where it was put on a timber frame or "hearse" and covered with a hearse-cloth. The coverings were frequently lent by the parish or, for those in better circumstances, a livery company; the Stationers' Company, had one "of cloth of gold powdered with blue velvet and bordered with black velvet, embroidered and stained with blue, red, yellow and green." But a parish would even accommodate the poorest of its flock; a record in the Lambeth archives notes "a sheet, to bury a poor man—12 d. … Laid next about the burial of a poor man that died in the wash way—2s.8d." Many parishes also had coffins they reused, putting the shrouded body in it until the corpse reached the gravesite for burial. In most cases, such burials took place in the churchyard, although some of the more affluent were buried within the church itself. The church of All Hallows Honey Lane, London, made additional space by housing the dead between the church floor and the ceiling of the cellar below (which was separately owned). If there was no more room in the parish ground, they were permitted to utilize the burial place attached to St. Paul's Cathedral.[33] There was also a paid position: the common practice of paying a bell-man to go around a parish between the death and the burial requesting the prayers of the people for the newly dead; his visits were also a sign for the poor and the local clergy to gather at the burial as well.[34] "And so," sighs Old Siward of his son who dies when Birnam Wood comes to Dunsinane Hill and the final battle in *Macbeth* occurs, "his knell is knoll'd" (5.9.16). Knowledge of the passing bell could also be hauntingly personal. In London in July 1607, Shakespeare's nephew Edward, "sonne of Edward [rightly Edmund] Shackspeere Player base born"[35] was baptized at St. Leonard's parish; a month later, he was buried at Cripplegate. And then, barely five months after that, Shakespeare's brother Edmund was buried at St. Saviour's Church, Southwark, on December 31, at the age of 27; William Shakespeare is thought to have paid for the great bell being rung there for him (Honan, p. 230), perhaps the "surly sullen bell" of Shakespeare's sonnet 71, which "Give[s] warning to the world that I am fled From this vile world with vildest worms to dwell" (3-4). It was less than two years after Shakespeare had composed *Macbeth*. And fellow players followed: William Sly on August 16, and Lawrence Fletcher on September 12, both less than a year later.

Still, those dreaded bells were not the ones dreaded most of all. Those were what Ben Jonson's *Volpone* calls "The bells in time of pestilence" that "ne'er made Like noise" (3.5.5–6).[36] It was said that an ox tolled the bell at Woolwich to signal the plague of 1593. Such epidemics in Shakespeare's England were unexpected, random, and devastating. They were also frequent: plague struck in the year of Elizabeth's coronation, 1558; in 1563 it struck again, killing nearly one quarter of the population of London; and the epidemic returned roughly every four years until 1582; then again in 1593 and 1597; and in 1603, delaying James's coronation, just two years before *Macbeth*. Some thought it was caused by bad air. Timon refers to "a planetary plague, when Jove Will o'er some high-vic'd city hang poison In the sick air" (4.3.109–11). Others blamed the conjunction of planets. In *Troilus and Cressida*, Ulysses observes that "when the planets In evil mixture to disorder wander, What plagues and what portents, what Mutiny!" (1.3.94–96). Thomas Nashe has inscribed what the plague was like in unforgettable detail:

> All day and all night long car-men did nothing but go up and down the streets with their carts and cry "Have you any dead to bury? Have you any dead to bury?" and had many times out of one house their whole loading. One grave was the sepulchre of seven score, one bed was the altar whereon whole families were offered.
>
> The walls were hoared and furred with the moist scorching steam of their desolation. Even as, before a gun is shot off, a stinking smoke funnels out and prepares the way for him, so before any gave up the ghost, death, arrayed in a stinking smoke, sopped his nostrils and crammed itself full into his mouth that close up his fellow's eyes, to give him warning to prepare for his funeral. Some died sitting at their meat, others as they were asking counsel of the physician for their friends. I saw at the house where I was hosted, a maid bring her master warm broth for to comfort him, and she sink down dead herself ere he had half eat it up.[37]

Elsewhere, he is more succinct:

> Beauty is but a flowre,
> Which wrinckles will devoure,
> Brightnesse falls from the ayre,
> Queenes have died yong, and faire,
> Dust hath closed Helens eye.
> I am sick, I must dye,
> Lord have mercy on us.[38]

"What disease is there in the world so venonmous in infecting, so full of pain in suffering, so hasty in devouring, and so difficult in curing, as the plague is?" asks Thomas Phaire in *The Regiment of Life* (1560). The General Orders issued against the plague in 1592 did suggest some cures: dried rosemary, juniper, bayleaves, or frankincense burned and carried about the house. Housewives were urged to keep on hand rue and herb of grace. Face in Ben Jonson's *The Alchemist* burns rose-vinegar, treacle, and tar (5.1). But the best protection was thought to be three or four peeled onions left on the ground for ten days to gather the neighborhood's infection: Sir Politic Would-be in Jonson's *Volpone* suggests blowing air on sliced onions as a test:

> Now, sir, your onion, which doth naturally
> Attract th' infection, and your bellows, blowing
> The air upon him, will show instantly
> By his changed color if there be contagion,
> Or else remain as fair as at the first (4.1.121–26).

The plague killed more men than women, perhaps because rats, which we now know carried fleas with the disease, inhabited the granaries, docks, and warehouses where they worked. The disease was so contagious (and nearly always fatal) that those who were ill were quarantined; by 1568 any house where a plague victim lived was shut up for at least twenty days, with the sick and all other members of the household shut inside, a "paper" nailed to the outside door showing a red cross and the tell-tale petition, "Lord, have mercy on us," warning others to stay away. It was the beadle's job to see that infected houses were properly marked and that, in the wintertime, lantern and candlelight were hung at every doorway. The oaths of constables, meanwhile, required them to report to the Lord Mayor the true number of those who died in their precincts and to arrest those wandering and idle persons who might transport the sickness. The two churchwardens and clerk of each parish were responsible for proper house inspections and burials, but in the course of Shakespeare's lifetime, the parish churchyards were filled up. In 1582, 23 parishes drew on land in St. Paul's Churchyard so that no new graves could be dug without exposing those previously buried. In other poor and overcrowded parishes, dead bodies were merely covered with a winding-sheet and dropped into pest-pits; Thomas Dekker records that, during the 1603 plague epidemic, bodies tumbled "into their ever-lasting lodgings (ten in one heape, and twenty in another) .... The gallant and the beggar lay together; the scholler and the carter in one bed."[39] We can sense the dread of the plague-bell from George Wither's commentary:

“Have you any dead [illegible]
Whole housholds, and whole streets are stricken,
The sick to die, the sound do sicken,
And Lord have mercy upon us, crying
Ere Mercy can come forth, th’are dying.
No musick now is heard but bells,
And all their tunes are sick mens knells;
And every stroake the bell does toll,
Up to heaven it windes a soule.[40]

The sound of the ringing bell in *Macbeth* leads to testimony from Macduff —“O horror, horror, horror! Tongue nor heart Cannot conceive nor name thee” (2.3.64-65)—but he goes on to record just what he has seen. The plague-bell on the charnel wagons announced horrors confirmed by Bills of Mortality. Begun in 1552, these were weekly documents and many are still extant. Parish clerks had a regular system in place by 1555; in 1563, John Stow saw records listing 20,136 plague deaths. In 1593, Richard Stoneley, a minor civil servant, noted in his diary that “of the whole year from the 21 of December 1592 to 20 December 1593—Died of all diseases, 16,844, whereof the plague is 10,662. Christened this year 4,021. Parishes clear of the plague—none.” From December 23, 1602, to December 22, 1603, 38,244 people died, 30,578 of the plague. Such figures, writes Liza Picard,

> were collated from returns made by the “Viewers” or “Searchers” of the dead: two old women who might otherwise be on parish relief, employed to go to any house where a death had

> been notified to the parish clerk … . Their diagnosis was based on experience—they would certainly recognize a plague death… . They must have been walking foci of infection themselves, which was why they had to put their reports in a box at the foot of the stairs in the Stationers' Company's hall … . They were paid by the parish, 2d. a body. [41]

No widespread epidemic occurs in *Macbeth*, but Macduff's report to Malcolm makes the widespread slaughter under the tyrannical Macbeth similar. Macduff reports to the self-exiled Malcolm that

> Each new morn
> New widows howl, new orphans cry, new sorrows
> Strike heaven on the face, that it resounds
> As if it felt with Scotland, and yell'd out
> Like syllable of dolor (4.3.4–8).

Rosse confirms such a message. Scotland, he says,

> where nothing,
> But who knows nothing, is once seen to smile;
> Where sighs, and groans, and shrieks that rent the air
> Are made not mark'd, where violent sorrow seems
> A modern ecstasy,

and then seems to draw the analogy tighter with both the passing bell and the bell of the charnel wagon resonating:

> The dead man's knell
> Is there scarce ask'd for who, and good men's lives
> Expire before the flowers in their caps,
> Dying or ere they sicken (4.3.166–75).

The bell of death and the bell of epidemic seem to ring in Act 4 of Shakespeare's play.

Such bells "Ne'er ring well till they are at their full pitch," Flamineo informs Marcello in John Webster's *The White Devil* (1612; 3.3.31).[42] Such bells are still another kind of bell that can have cognitive bearing on the bell Macbeth hears before he proceeds to kill Duncan. It is the alarum bell that denotes pitched battle: such a bell is heard relentlessly in the battle of Corioles (*Coriolanus* 1.4.9,19,29,43,47; 1.5.3). But the alarum bell that Macduff rings in *Macbeth* to call the castle's occupants to account is more serious; it is the bell that in Shakespeare's time would denote to the playgoers at the Globe an act of treason. This is what Geoffrey Bullough has in mind when he compares the alarum bell at Inverness to the "tolling of the bell of the Palace-clock" in Paris that Queen Catherine uses to signal the great St. Bartholomew's Day Massacre of the Huguenots in 1572. Bullough cites several parallels found in the account of the bloody, savage massacre found in the *Illustris Viri Iac. August Thuami… Historiarium sui Temporis 1543–1607*:

> The Queen, fearing lest the King, whom she thought she did observe, still wavering and staggering at the horridness of the enterprize, should change his mind, comes into his Bed chamber at midnight, whither presently Anjou, Nevers, Biragus, Tavannes, Radesianus, and after them Guise, came by agreement. There they immind [were put in mind of] the King, hesitating, and after a long discourse had to and fro, upbraided by his Mother, that by his delaying he would let slip a fair occasion offered him by God, of subduing his enemies. By which speech the King, finding himself accused of Cowardise, and being of himself of a fierce nature, and accustomed to bloud-shed, was inflamed, and gave command to put the thing in execution. Therefore the Queen, laying hold of his present heat, lest by delaying it should slack, commands that the sign which was to have been given at break of day should be hastened, and that the Bell of the nearer Church of St. German Auxerrois should be tolled.

Bullough comments, "The reverberations of that bell were heard by Protestants for generations. Moreover it was widely reported that Charles IX suffered great remorse, sleeplessness and hallucinations after the slaughter. There is no need to believe that Shakespeare consciously recalled St. Bartholomew. His alarm bell is rung after the murder, and would be found in most castles. Macbeth's remorse is based on Kenneth's and needs no other source. Yet the possibility remains."[43]

But there is a stark difference: Macduff calls forth his companions to what he perceives as Doomsday—but he pointedly omits Macbeth. His vision—his mind's eye—is realized on stage, against the clanging of the great bell, as the occupants of the castle pour forth in their white nightclothes, resembling representations of the Last Judgment common in Tudor art. They are stripped of armor and of weapons, horribly vulnerable. Lady Macbeth is the first to comment, not, as we might expect, Banquo or Malcolm or Donalbain. "What's the business?" she demands, "That such a hideous trumpet calls to parley The sleepers of the house?" and, when, told—"O gentle lady … . Our royal master's murther'd!"—her quick reflex—"What, in our house?"—conflates her castle and her lineage, both her "houses." Only then does Macbeth enter, accompanied by the newcomers Lennox and Rosse. But rather than displaying alarm, he shows a sudden resignation.

> Had I but died an hour before this chance,
> I had liv'd a blesséd time; for from this instant
> There's nothing serious in mortality:
> All is but toys; renown and grace is dead,
> The wine of life is drawn, and the mere lees,
> Is left this vault to brag of (2.3.81–96).

He verbally stresses Doomsday, what may also be in the minds' eyes of Shakespeare's original playgoers.

It is as if Macbeth is overcome with the ringing of great bells that have marked their fruitless treason in recent English history: the ringing of bells in 1569 to raise northern Catholics in rebellion and, later, to warn the rebel Earl of Northumberland to escape; the bells that proclaimed the Parry plot against Elizabeth in 1585 and again, a year later, at the unraveling of the Catholic conspiracy in the discovery of the Babington Plot; and still again in 1587 to proclaim the beheading of Mary Stuart, Queen of Scots, Elizabeth's rival claimant to the English throne. Even Simon Eyre's innocent pancake bell would come, in the later years of Elizabeth and those of James, to proclaim not merely the freedom of apprentices on Shrove Tuesday, but a holiday that could represent their own anarchic rebellions and mob rule. John Taylor the Water Poet records of Shrove Tuesday 1617 that

> all the whole Kingdome is in quiet, but by that time the clocke strikes eleuen, which (by the helpe of a knavish Sexton) is commonly before nine, then there is a bell rung, cald The Pancake Bell, the sound whereof makes thousands of people distracted, and forgetfull either of manner or humanitie.[44]

These riots could be marked by tearing down houses thought to be brothels, carting prostitutes through the streets, freeing prisoners from local jails, and attacking the theaters.

There are not one, but two, "alarm" bells in *Othello,* the slightly earlier play that seems in ways to have stood as a working model for *Macbeth.* Iago initiates both of them, the success of the first doubtless inspiring the second. The first instance is in Venice, where he arouses Desdemona's father Brabantio and the city to reveal her act of carnality: "Arise, arise!" he shouts, "Awake the snorting citizens with the bell, Or the devil will make a grandsire of you. Arise, I say!" for "Even now, now, very now, an old black ram Is tupping your white ewe" (1.1.89–92, 88–89). Later, on Cyprus, with the town left in charge of Iago's rival Cassio, when the bell strikes eleven (2.2.10), Iago rings the alarm bell to halt the fight between Cassio and Roderigo in which Montano is wounded. "For Christian shame," Othello tells his men,

> put by this barbarous brawl,
> He that stirs next to carve for his own rage
> Holds his soul light; he dies upon his motion.
>
> And then,
>
> Silence that dreadful bell, it frights the isle
> From her propriety (2.3.172–76).

Both Iago's betrayal of Cassio and Othello and Macbeth's assassination of Duncan are what Banquo would term acts of "treasonous malice" (2.3.132). The alarm that summons the household at Inverness after Duncan's death is discovered is echoed in the alarm bell that summons Macduff to his duel with Macbeth in the play's last battle (5.8.8). But it is not the final alarm bell in the play of *Macbeth*: that sound rings, another "dreadful bell," as Macduff exits fighting Macbeth only to reenter and exit once again, carrying Macbeth's bloody head (5.8.34). There has been another act of treason, another change of rule, another Doomsday. Bells thus carve out Macbeth's career in Shakespeare's accounting of it—from the handbell that invites him to kill the King to the alarum bell that rings out his own death in turn. Together they issue forth the soundscape of bells that, rather than being the "sound and fury" that "Signif[ies] nothing" (5.5.27–28), signifies everything in the play, bringing an entire cultural range of sound, along varying neural pathways in the mind's ear, to various playgoers at the defining moments of Shakespeare's play.

SHAKESPEARE'S WILLS

Absent wills and present heirs abound in Shakespeare; unseen documents whose contents remain unknown direct characters we meet. *All's Well That Ends Well* opens abruptly with Bertram; his mother; Helena; and Lord Lafew, the French King's messenger, all dressed in the black of mourning, all confronting the consequence of the death and the legacy of the Count of Rossillion. Bertram has assumed his father's title, but he is in his minority and so the title has passed on to the King, who holds him in wardship until he reaches the age of twenty-one. His mother, the Countess of Rossillion, feels the double loss; she tells Lafew, "In delivering my son from me, I bury a second husband" (1.1.1–2). For young Bertram the loss is worse yet. His mourning for his father renewed, he now also mourns for his own immediate situation: "And I in going, madam, weep o'er my father's death anew; but I must attend his Majesty's command, to whom I am now in ward, evermore in subjection" (1.1.3–5). The escalation of his language first grounded in *weep—command, ward, subjection*—reveals his state of mind; he has not only lost a father and a title, but he has inherited servitude. Neither he nor his mother has any choice in the matter, any means of appeal. Lafew attempts to ameliorate the situation by responding to family loss: "You shall find of the King a husband, madam, and you, sir, a father" (1.1.6–7). Bertram's father had the title and gift of Rossillion, a former province in southern France just north of the eastern end of the Pyrenees, in exchange for military service, but Bertram's newly inherited conscription is not his decision. His father should have died hereafter. Now, instead, "My thanks and duty are your Majesty's" (1.2.23). As Bertram is keenly aware, the King as his guardian by law controls his property and can even arrange his marriage and, thus, his indefinite future. By holding his inheritance, the King with his command supersedes his father's will.

The practice of wardships in England goes back to the years just after the Norman Conquest and continued into Shakespeare's time. As B.J. Sokol and Mary Sokol recount,

> Although wardship arose in the case of land held by socage (agricultural) tenure or by military tenure (knight service or grand serjeanty), it was most onerous in military tenure. … [In such cases,] once wardship began the lord took all the ward's land under his control and was entitled to keep all the profits from the land for the duration of the wardship. In theory the lord was supposed to be liable for any waste, or damage to the heir's land, but in practice few heirs had sufficient cash assets available when they came of age to allow them to pursue an action for waste.[1]

The terms of wardship were not concluded until the ward reached majority, but in military tenure the ward could still not take possession of his lands until he applied formally by means of a procedure known as "sue his livery" (as in *Richard II*, 2.1.22–24, 2.3.129) if, as in the case of Bertram as tenant-in-chief, the guardian was the king. Such a procedure was long and meant an investigation into the heir's landholding; most heirs avoided it by paying the king an amount of money instead. But, in addition, the lord (or king) was entitled to a fine of half a year's profit from the land when the ward reached majority. Furthermore, the lord also controlled the ward's body during the period of wardship. He could determine where the ward lived and how, being responsible for the ward's daily needs and the ward's education, training, and marriage. Statutes of 1236 and 1275 permitted heirs to refuse marriages proposed by their guardians, but, if they did, they paid for rejecting the plan with heavy financial fines; and if the heir married without license from the lord, the lord was then entitled to a compensation amounting to double the value of the marriage and was further entitled to continue to take profit from the land until he had received that payment. In 1540, Henry VIII instituted a Court of Wards to centralize and control the sale of wardships, raising state revenues and consolidating royal social control. But purchases of wardships became profitable investments, especially if wards with land or fortunes could be married off during their wardships, in some cases to the children of the guardians themselves. Gloucester is enraged in *King Lear* when his bastard son Edmund tells him that, "I have heard [Edgar] oft maintain it to be fit that, sons at perfect age and fathers declin'd, the father should be as ward to the son, and the son manage his revenue" (1.2.71–74).

Such widespread practices led to widespread abuses in the world of Shakespeare's playgoers. We can begin to measure Bertram's anxiety—as well as the somber, melancholy mood of the opening scene of *All's Well*—when we note instances of wardship contemporary with Shakespeare's play that have been gathered by Lawrence Stone:

> A particularly striking case is that of Walter Aston, son and heir of Sir Edward Aston. In 1597 he was sold at the official price of £300 to Sir Edward Coke, the Attorney-General. But in addition to this official payment, Coke had to give Lord Burghley [the head of the Court of Wards] no less than £1,000, so that he had invested heavily in the purchase of the child. When in 1600 the boy secretly married one Anne Barnes, Coke was naturally enraged; Anne was put in the Fleet [prison] for nearly a year, and the marriage was dissolved by the Court of High Commission. But the boy had spirit and determination and soon afterwards he again married against Coke's will, for which he had to pay his odious guardian £4,000 … . In 1609 Richard, son and heir to the Earl of Dorset, was hastily married off two days before his father's death so as to forestall the Duke of Lennox who was fishing for the wardship, and when the Earl of Pembroke was thought to be at death's door in 1595 it was reported that "the tribe of Hunsdon doe laye waite for the wardship of the brave yong lord."[2]

"Men invested in these commodities like any other," Stone comments wryly, "in the hope of financial gain or political advantage, and they were rarely disappointed" (p. 601).

In *The Scourge of Villanie* (1598), the satirist John Marston sees the potential cruelty and immorality of wardship as the loss of freedom:

> Bondslaves sonnes had wont be bought & sold;
> But now Heroes heires (if they have not told
> A discreet number, for theyr dad did die)
> Are made much of: how much mercandie?

> Tail'd and retail'd, till like the pedlar's packe
> The fourth-hand ward-ware comes, alack, alack.[3]

Bertram has much the same feeling of confinement upon arriving at court. "I am commanded here, and kept a coil with," he complains to Parolles, "'Too young' and 'the next year' and "tis too early' … . I shall stay here the forehorse to a smock, Creaking my shoes on the plain masonry, Till honor be bought up, and no sword worn But one to dance with!" (2.1.27–33). But Marston and Bertram were not alone. The House of Commons, noting similar abuses, proposed abolishing the Court of Wards and Liveries in 1598 and renewed their efforts under James in 1604, along with the elimination of the institution of wardship itself; not coincidentally, this is the time (1602–1604) that Shakespeare was writing *All's Well That Ends Well*. Luke Wilson records a similarly broad literary discontent among playwrights: "most notoriously George Wilkins in *The Miseries of Enforced Marriage* (1607), but also Thomas Neale in *The Ward* (1637), … Jonson in *The Staple of News* (1626), and, of course, in *Bartholomew Fair* [1614]. *Bartholomew Fair* is peculiar because both parties to the premised marriage—not only Grace [Wellborn] but [Bartholomew] Cokes too—are or seem to be, or to have been, wards. … Wardship takes the place of the typical blocking figure: it poses the single most definite problem the play sets out to solve."[4] Wardship is the fundamental blocking device in *All's Well*, too. Whatever Bertram's father drew up as Count of Rossillion, assuming he would live until Bertram came of age, was abrogated by the King of France and his practice of wardships. Bertram, we recall, would "weep o'er my father's death anew; but I must attend his Majesty's command, to whom I am now in ward, evermore in subjection" (1.1.3–5).

With Helena, the circumstances are somewhat different than they are for Bertram but, like Portia in *The Merchant of Venice*, Helena finds (in the words of Portia), "the will of a living daughter" subject to "the will of a dead father" (*Merchant*, 1.2.24–25). Both Helena and Portia must determine how to work within the legacies of their fathers. "If Portia were to marry outside the terms of her father's will," Sokol and Sokol write, "she would lose not only ease and wealth, but also her standing as the great lady of Belmont" (p. 63). The will that Portia manages to construe to her own benefit begins when she warmly welcomes Bassanio, continues when she encourages him to "tarry, pause a day or two" (3.2.1), and concludes when she gives him a hint to choose the lead casket by requesting a song with words that rhyme with *lead* (3.2.63–72). Although we never hear of the terms of the will directly except through Portia's waiting-gentlewoman Nerissa (1.2.27–33), we can see Portia executing the will so that she achieves the outcome she desires. We can make deductions concerning the absent will of Helena's father similar to the ones we make with Portia's father and with Bertram's father. The first involves Helena's position. She is the "sole child" of Gerard de Narbon (1.1.38) who is "bequeathed to [the Countess of Rossillion's] overlooking" (1.1.38–39; 1.3.101–02). Just as Portia's father has made certain in his will that she will, given the caskets and their hidden objects and messages, receive a suitor most desirable for her, Helena's father has arranged a way to care for his daughter. Gerard de Narbon has willed Helena a special knowledge of his medicine. While William Gouge's *Of Domesticall Duties* (1622) allowed widows to inherit household goods—personal chattels, such as the iron mortar and pestle, the kettle, and the pewter dish Mary Dod of Cheshire claimed, stage properties we do not see, under the law of coverture[5]—a father can will his medical secrets—an intangible we cannot see—in a will to his daughter that never appears on stage. "You know," Helena tells the Countess,

> my father left me some prescriptions
> Of rare and prov'd effects, such as his reading
> And manifest experience had collected
> For general sovereignty; and that he will'd me
> In heedfull'st reservation to bestow them,
> As notes whose faculties inclusive were
> More than they were in note. Amongst the rest,
> There is a remedy, approv'd, set down,
> To cure the desperate languishings whereof
> The King is render'd lost (1.3.221–30).

What Helena most wants—association with Bertram and now a reason to journey to Paris (ostensibly to cure the King) to see him once more—are provided for her by her father's will, "the will of the dead father" now reinforcing "the will of a living daughter." Earlier, Lafew himself seems to have recognized the potential significance of her particular inheritance: "You must hold the credit of your father," he tells her on his departure for Paris with Bertram (1.1.78). "Helena's task [is] not that of a servant," Sheldon Zitner writes, "but an inheritor."[6] Now her father's "good receipt," she tells the Countess, "Shall for my legacy be sanctified By th' luckiest stars in heaven, and would your honor But give me leave to try success, I'd venture The well-lost of mine on his Grace's cure By such a day, such an hour" (1.3.244–49). Her father's will gives Helena a public purpose to go to court; and it gives her the

Countess' blessing as well: "What I can help thee to," she tells Helena, "thou shalt not miss" (1.3.256).

Just as Portia translates the terms of her father's will into the conquest of Bassanio for her husband, so Helena translates her father's legacy into the means to secure the recalcitrant Bertram for herself. "My art is not past power," she tells the King of France once she joins the court in Paris, "nor you past cure" (2.1.158). Thus, accustomed to the benefits of her legacy, Helena turns the possibility of curing the King of his fistula into her desire to win Bertram. Armed with the knowledge her father left her, Helena strikes a bargain with the King.

Helena: If I break time, or flinch in property
Of what I spoke, unpitied let me die,
And well deserve'd. Not helping, death's my foe,
But if I help, what do you promise me?
King: Make thy demand.
Helena: But will you make it even?
King: Ay, by my sceptre and my hopes of [heaven].
Helena: Then shalt thou give me with thy kingly hand
What husband in thy power I will command (2.1.187-94).

Her father's gift will not prove excessive, and she will not be excessive in her reward. "Exempted be from me the arrogance To choose from forth the royal blood of France," she replies by way of refinement: "My low and humble name to propagate With any branch or image of thy state; But such a one thy vassal, whom I know Is free for me to ask, thee to bestow" (2.1.195–200). The word *vassal* can well give the game away, for it best describes Bertram's new condition. But the King is as extravagant in his response to their bargain as Helena is in establishing it. The King orders Lafew to call forth the lords in his court. "Fair maid" he tells her, "send forth thine eye. This youthful parcel Of noble bachelors stand at my bestowing, O'er whom both sovereign power and father's voice I have to use." They are an assembly of wards. "Thy frank election make; Thou hast power to choose, and they none to forsake" (2.3.52–56). This scene too resembles *The Merchant of Venice*; we know in advance Helena's choice just as we know Portia's, and the ritual of selection is essentially an artificial one. And like Portia, she makes disparaging remarks about each prospective suitor until she comes to Bertram. But she does not "choose" him; rather, "I give me and my service, ever whilst I live, Into your guiding power" (2.3.102–04): seeing Bertram in a position of abjection, she transfers a new sense of power to him. But he will not have her.

Bertram: My wife, my liege? I shall beseech your Highess,
In such a business, give me leave to use
The help of mine own eyes.
King: Know'st thou not, Bertram,
What she has done for me?
Bertram: Yes, my good lord,
But never hope to know why I should marry her.
King: Thou know'st she has rais'd me from my sickly bed.
Bertram: But follows it, my lord, to bring me down
Must answer for your raising? I know her well;
She had her breeding at my father's charge—
A poor physician's daughter my wife! Disdain
Rather corrupt me ever! (2.3.106–16)

Bertram recognizes the proposed alliance as disparagement, the legal term for the imposition of gross misalliances of rank against which wards can claim nominal legal protection. The King stiffens, and mounts a kind of counterattack. "'Tis only title thou disdain'st in her, the which I can build up" (2.3.117–18). Raising Helen's social status enlarges upon Gerard de Narbon's legacy—as with Bertram's father, the King manages to trump the inheritance of the parent—but at the same time, it makes the Count of Rossillion's legacy to Bertram the more terribly confining. The potentialities of one will underscore the limitations of the other. Bertram is once again defeated by the King's command. Evermore in subjection, he turns reluctantly to Helena.

I shall obey his will.
You must not marvel, Helen, at my course,
Which holds not color with the time, nor does
The ministration and required office
On my particular. Prepar'd I was not
For such a business; therefore am I found
So much unsettled. This drives me to entreat you
That presently you take your way for home,
And rather muse than ask why I entreat you,
For my respects are better than they seem,
And my appointments have in them a need
Greater than shows itself at the first view
To you that know them not (2.5.57-69).

He undergoes the wedding ceremony but he flees its consummation, his father's foreshortened life reflected in his foreshortened marriage.

Bertram's response thus also foreshortens the possibilities inherent in the legacy Gerard de Narbon left on behalf of his daughter.

Bertram's deep desire—and his need—for the liberty of majority has already been introduced in Helena's desire—and hope—for marriage to Bertram; and she construes a philosophy that will permit it, as well as a specific plan: "Our remedies oft in ourselves do lie, Which we ascribe to heaven. The fated sky Gives me free scope, only doth backward pull Our slow designs when we ourselves are dull … . The King's disease—my project may deceive me, But my intents are fix'd, and will not leave me" (1.1.216–29). Surprisingly in this class-conscious play (and oddly, perhaps, in a time when the Court of Wards and Liveries was under siege), the King supports her.

> Strange is it that our bloods,
> Of color, weight, and heat, pour'd all together,
> Would quite confound distinction, yet stands off
> In difference so mighty. If she be
> All that is virtuous—save what thou dislik'st,
> A poor physician's daughter—thou dislik'st
> Of virtue for the name. But do not so.
> From lowest place [when] virtuous things proceed,
> The place is dignified by th' doer's deed. …
> If thou canst like this creature as a maid,
> I can create the rest. Virtue and she
> Is her own dower; honor and wealth from me (2.3.118-44).

The use of royal prerogative to transform class in order to reinforce the possibilities of wardship for the guardian is a powerful action; done in the name of virtue and honor it upholds those two qualities that the Countess has already used to describe both Bertram and Helena (1.1.42–43; 1.1.62). Together, then, the four principal characters of *All's Well That Ends Well* question the validity (and utility) of unseen wills on present circumstances. And together they disclose what elsewhere Lloyd Davis has called the essential "instability of the inheritance" system in Shakespeare's time.[7]

Even more frequently than blurring class distinctions, wills upholding the limitations of primogeniture were interrogated by the playwrights of the time. Orlando is especially vexed and vocal at the start of *As You Like It*. He tells his first-born brother Oliver,

> I know you are my eldest brother, and in the gentle condition of blood you should know me. The courtesy of nations allows you

> my better, in that you are the first born, but the same tradition takes not away my blood, were there twenty brothers betwixt us. I have as much of my father in me as you, albeit I confess your coming before me is nearer to his reverence. … My father charg'd you in his will to give me good education. You have train'd me like a peasant, obscuring the hiding from me all gentleman-like qualities. The spirit of my father grows strong in me, and I will no longer endure it; therefore allow me such exercises as may become a gentleman, or give me the poor allottery my father left me by testament, with that I will go buy my fortune (1.1.44–51; 67–74).

In George Chapman's *The Widdowes Teares* (c. 1605; published 1612) Thrasalio tells his older brother Lysander, "you were too forward when you stepped into the world before me, and gulled me of the land that my spirits and parts were indeed born to" (1.1.45–47).[8] Primogeniture was also problematic when the eldest son was a bastard, as in the case of Philip in *King John* (1.1.49–83). Still a third problem raised by wills occurs when the inheritance itself is tainted, as in *The Pvritaine or The Widow of Watling-street* (1607). Here the grieving widow Lady Plus confesses to her son Master Edmond that his father "would deceaue all the world to get riches for thee" (1.1.52–53), an action Edmund intends to emulate: "he cozn'd the right heire, beeing a foole, and bestow'd those Lands vpon me his eldest Son. … Why, al the world knowes, as long as twas his pleasure to get me, twas his duety to get for me: I know the law in that point; no Atturney can gull me . … I know what I may do well inough by my Fathers Copy: the Lawe's in mine owne hands now: nay, now I know my strength" (1.1.174–86).[9]

As *All's Well That Ends Well* makes clear—wellness meaning health of body and mind; justice in distributing rewards; equity in fashioning exceptions to the rule—the creation, execution, and administration of wills could be extremely troubled in Shakespeare's rapidly changing culture. So, too, the very concept of inheritance—of willing something—was troubled. Inheritance, for instance, was held out as a promise or bargain, as Petruchio fashions it in advancing his claim for Kate in *The Taming of the Shrew*:

> Signior Baptista, my business asketh haste,
> And every day I cannot come to woo.
> You knew my father well, and in him me,
> Left soly heir to all his lands and goods,
> Which I have bettered rather than decreas'd.

Then tell me, if I get your daughter's love,
What dowry shall I have with her to wife? (2.1.114–20),

followed by Tranio (disguised as Lucentio) in suing for Bianca:

Sir, list to me:
I am my father's heir and only son.
If I may have your daughter to my wife,
I'll leave her houses three or four as good,
Within rich Pisa walls, as any one
Old Signior Gremio has in Padua,
Besides two thousand ducats by the year
Of fruitful land, all which shall be her jointer (2.1.363–70).

Timon of Athens makes much the same kind of proposal—what is enough, in this instance, rather than what is competitively necessary—in advancing the cause of his loyal servant Lucilius:

Timon: How shall she be endowed,
If she is mated with an equal husband?
Old Athenian: Three talents on the present; in future, all.
Timon: This gentleman of mine hath serv'd me long;
To build his fortune, I will strain a little,
For 'tis a bond in men. Give him thy daughter;
What you bestow, in him I'll counterpoise,
And make him weigh with her (1.1.139-46).

Living wills, in such cases, serve to guarantee present inheritances. Conversely, present wills could also serve as threats. Aaron is fierce: "He dies upon my scimitar's sharp point, That touches my first-born son and heir!" (*Titus Andronicus*, 4.2.91–92). Old Capulet can be cruel to his daughter Juliet:

And you be mine, I'll give you to my friend;
And you be not, hang, beg, starve, die in the streets,
For, by my soul, I'll ne'er acknowledge thee,
Nor what is mine shall never do thee good.
Trust to it, bethink you, I'll not be forsworn (3.5.191–95),

his case for Paris the will of a living father upon the will of a living daughter. Master Page reverses the role in *The Merry Wives of Windsor*, using his powers to define inheritance not to force a marriage but to prevent one. But in addressing Anne's plan to marry Fenton, his remarks are gentler:

> Not by my consent, I promise you. The gentleman is of no having. He kept company with the wild Prince and Poins; he is of too high a region, he knows too much. No, he shall not knit a knot in his fortunes with the finger of my substance. If he take her, let him take her simply. The wealth I have waits on my consent, and my consent goes not that way (3.2.71–78).

Egeus would exercise the same powers in *A Midsummer Night's Dream*, but his extensive argument to Duke Theseus of Athens in defense of his position suggests that he has some reservations about the strength of his case and his authority over Hermia:

> Stand forth, Demetrius. My noble lord,
> This man hath my consent to marry her.
> Stand forth, Lysander. And, my gracious Duke,
> This man hath bewitch'd the bosom of my child. …
> And, my gracious Duke,
> Be it so she will not here before your Grace
> Consent to marry with Demetrius.
> I beg the ancient privilege of Athens:
> As she is mine, I may dispose of her;
> Which shall be either to this gentleman,
> Or to her death, according to our law
> Immediately provided in that case (1.1.24–45).

His sense of bewilderment and injury anticipates that of Brabantio and his appeal to the Venetian senate: his resorting to the inexplicable as caused by the bewitchment of Desdemona is much the same (*Othello*, 1.3.60-64), so that there can be little wonder that the King of France feels affronted by Bertram's disobedience. He finds it an action that is both personal and public: "My honor's at the stake, which to defeat, I must produce my power. Here, take her hand, Proud scornful boy, unworthy this good gift, That dost in vile misprision shackle up My love and her desert" (2.3.149–53). Enforcing the will of Helena, the King empowers the will of Gerard de Narbon and, in regaining his authority, he fulfills the responsibility that is his following the early death of the Count of Rossillion. All these plays rest on the characters' cognition and the cognition of the playgoers, on the rights and pitfalls of making out and administering wills.

Indeed, "by Shakespeare's time," the Sokols write, "property could be willed away from an heir at any time." Their example is drawn from *The Two Noble Kinsmen* and the subplot of the Jailer's Daughter:

> This young woman has a father unhappy about the scant dowry he can offer. Yet her unnamed Wooer is content to marry with no more than a promise of future consideration in her father's will . . . . But then the daughter falls desperately in love with Palamon, and risks releasing him from prison. Even this desperate act does not win her his love, and so she goes mad. Subsequently Palamon obtains the Jailer's and his daughter's pardons, and
>
> > Now to be held ungrateful to her goodness,
> > Has given a sum of money to her marriage—
> > A large one, I'll assure you. (*TNK* 4.1.22–4)
>
> So then the daughter has a dowry and a steadfast Wooer, but not the sanity that would make marriage possible. Sexual healing is prescribed by the wise Doctor, and then marriage with the loyal Wooer arranged. Finally Palamon and his three kinsmen knights bequeath their purses "to piece her portion."
>
> The fable of chivalry in this play does not preclude a quite realistic mirroring of help given to a poor but worthy girl to "piece" her dowry, for dowries were on occasion charitably "pieced out" by well-wishing masters or local notables (p. 60)

and they further note *All's Well That Ends Well* is another play in which wills and dowries are made fluid in a power structure that undermined regulations with exceptions. But, by then in his career, Shakespeare had long since written history plays where dramatizations of the Tudor chronicles had rendered customary wills and inheritance arbitrary. Bullingbrook challenges the loss of his rightful estates (from his perspective) in *Richard II*: "I am a subject, And I challenge law. Attorneys are denied me, And therefore personally I lay my claim To my inheritance of free descent," Bullingbrook proclaims (2.3.133–36). Henry VI asks York, "may not a king adopt an heir?" and then adds, "If he may, then am I lawful king; For Richard, in the view of many lords, Resign'd the crown to Henry the Fourth, Whose heir my father was, and I am his" (*3 Henry VI*, 1.1.135–40). His fragile rule gives impetus to the rebel Jack Cade with his tattered mob: "It is to you, good people, that I speak, Over whom, in time to come, I hope to reign. For I am rightful heir unto this crown" (*2 Henry VI*, 4.2.129–31). In such creative (or capricious) circumstances, Helena can find her own holy reason to trick her way into recovering Bertram; she will offer herself to the Widow as a dower for her daughter Diana, a bold act of cognitive imagination, and then use Diana to secure Bertram's inherited ring:

> A ring the County wears,
> That downward hath succeeded in his house
> From son to son, some four or five descents,
> Since the first father wore it. This ring he holds
> In most rich choice, yet in his idle fire,
> To buy his will, it would not seem too dear,
> Howe'er repented after (3.7.22–28).

Her actions subvert Bertram's own intentions of enacting his inheritance and pave the way in the play for the braggart soldier Parolles to mock the making of wills altogether in his attempt to preserve his property (his life) from his apparent captors: "Sir, for a cardecue [a French coin worth two shillings]," he says, Bertram "will sell the fee-simple of his salvation, the inheritance of it, and cut th' entail from all remainders, and a perpetual succession for it perpetually" (4.3.278–81)—that is, renounce his own salvation and that of all his heirs' heirs, fee-simple being the nearest thing in English property law to absolute and perpetual possession, and entail the legal provision for establishing an estate to pass on successively to a series of predetermined heirs (278–81n.). In a world where wills can constantly be refashioned, they take on a kind of impermanence that can render any reliance on them mistaken. Shakespeare carries such possible cynicism as this to its greatest lengths in Pandarus' epilogue in *Troilus and Cressida*:

> Brethren and sisters of the hold-[door] trade,
> Some two months hence my will shall here be made.
> It should be now, but that my fear is this,
> Some galled goose of Winchester [prostitute] would hiss.
> Till then I'll sweat and seek about for eases,
> And at that time bequeath you my diseases (5.1.51-56),

his contagious syphilis the corollary dis-ease of random or indiscretionary inheritance.

Shakespeare and his fellow dramatists inhabit a world of potentially fraudulent wills. Old Flowerdale proposes just such a will confirming his deception in *The London Prodigall*, a text that is assigned to "William Shakespeare" on the title page of the 1605 quarto:

> presently weele goe and draw a will:
> Where weele set downe land that we neuer sawe,

And we will haue it of so large a summe,
Syr Lancelot shall intreat you take his daughter:
This being formed, giue it maister Weathercocke,
And make syr Lancelots daughter heire of all:
And make him sweare neuer to show the will
To any one, vntil that you be dead.
This done, the foolish changing Weathercocke
Will straight discourse vnto syr Lancelot
The forme and tenor of your Testament (2.1.152–62).[10]

Ben Jonson's Volpone is likewise deceptive. Subtitled, "The Fox," the play of *Volpone* shows how this Venetian "magnifico," with the aid of his "parasite" Mosca, gulls Voltore, Corbaccio, and Corvino, among others, to give him lavish gifts in the hopes of future compensation and more in his will. When Corbaccio inquires about the will, Volpone directs Mosca to "Show 'em a will. Open that chest and reach Forth one of those that has the blanks. I'll straight Put in thy name" (5.2.71–73).[11] The scene may have eerie echoes of Shakespeare's Antony during his funeral oration for the fallen Julius Caesar; holding out hope for all of Rome, he proclaims:

here's a parchment with the seal of Caesar,
I found it in his closet, 'tis his will.
Let but the commons hear this testament—
Which, pardon me, I do not mean to read—
And they would go and kiss dead Caesar's wounds,
And dip their napkins in his sacred blood;
Yea, beg a hair of him for memory,
And dying, mention it within their wills,
Bequeathing it as a rich legacy
Unto their issue (*Julius Caesar*, 3.2.128-37).

He puts it aside, only to pull it out again:

Here is the will, and under Caesar's seal:
To every Roman citizen he gives,
To every several man, seventy-five drachmaes. . . .
Moreover, he hath left you all his walks,
His private arbors and new-planted orchards,
On this side Tiber; he hath left them you,
And to your heirs for ever—common pleasures,
To walk abroad and recreate yourselves.

Here was a Caesar! when comes such another? (3.2.240-52)

But when the crowd asks for details—"The will, the will! we will hear Caesar's will" (3.2.139)—the word *will* punning on desire and document—Antony withholds it: "It is not meet you know how Caesar lov'd you" (3.2.141). Like Volpone's will, Caesar's parchment here may be blank. This present stage property—blank or not—creates a mutiny that will later transform the Roman republic into the Roman empire and begin its imperialist reach for greater world power. Here, it is a matter of inheritance, of wills, with effects far-reaching in historic time and geographic space. "But then," Park Honan, Shakespeare's biographer, tells us, "the poet's concern with inheritance—which [also] links *Macbeth* and *King Lear*—runs unusually deep. He shows in these works 'futures equivocally offered, by prediction and by action, as actualities,' notes a perceptive critic, 'and the disastrous attempt to impose limited designs upon the time of the world.' That does not quite impute to Shakespeare a moralistic aim, and Macbeth and Lear in turn are involved in nightmares of inheritance, and also in violently disruptive engagements, not only with time but with a civic polity and the inner self."[12]

Such practices breached the nature and intention of English wills; from the first extant examples in medieval times until well into the seventeenth century, wills were normally, if not exclusively, administered by the Church and with the Church's authority. "The will … was more than a way of disposing of property," Eamon Duffy comments. "It was in principle a religious document, the last opportunity to set one's fundamental religious orientation and orthodoxy solemnly on record before the confusions of the deathbed and the spiritual onslaught of demons … the two main religious preoccupations evident in the wills made before 1540 [were] almsgiving and prayers, [but] the essence of the deathbed pastoral care of the Church was to see that the Christian died in faith, hope, and charity. To die in charity meant, among other things, to die discharged of one's debts, and forgiving all injuries. Spiritual or material debts left undischarged would detain a soul in Purgatory, and it was a folkloric commonplace that the spirits of Purgatory might trouble the living till their debts were paid."[13] Duffy cites the case of Richard Hall of Bucknall who left a sheep worth twenty pence in 1512 to his parish priest "that he maie dispose it for the helthe of my soule as I have shewed him in confession" and gave the rest of his estate to his wife "to the paienge of my debtes and to dispose of the heyll of my soule as my executrix" (p. 356). To show how serious even small misdemeanors could be, Duffy cites a "London merchant who recalled how forty years before he had helped a kinsman in Derbyshire unjustly to seize a poor man's oxen 'in my wanton dayes whanne I lakkyd discrecyon': he asked his executors to trace the man or his executors and restore the cost of the beasts, or else to consult 'some sadde doctours of dyvynyte' to find the best way of spending the money 'for the wele of the soule of the said man ... and for the discharge of my conscien'" (p. 356). Duffy finds such remarks "relatively uncommon," however; "by far the most widespread expression of concern about spiritual indebtedness is to be found in the almost universal provision of bequests to the high altar of one's parish church" (p. 356).

In the time of Shakespeare the authority of making wills was prescribed in the Elizabethan *Book of Common Prayer*, which instructed men in good and poor health to declare their debts "for discharging of [their] conscience and quietness of [their] executours."[14] Shakespeare's family had good fortune in their legacies. His grandfather Richard left his father £38.17.0; his uncle Henry, a farmer, according to a witness, left "plenty of money in his coffers" and barns filled with corn and hay "of great value." Shakespeare's wife Anne inherited from her father £6.13.4, the equivalent of the annual wages of a blacksmith or a butcher.[15] E.A.J. Honigmann and Susan Brock record the will of Shakespeare's company's clown Robert Armin who "weake in bodie" in 1614, produces a preamble that, playing the Fool in *King Lear*, sounds remarkably like Lear himself:

> ffor the preventing of all controversies and contentions, which many tymes doe arise amongest deare ffrendes for the goodes and possessions of such as leave theire estates vndisposed of, being either prevented by sudden deaths or by protracting of tyme vntill such feeblenes and Debillitie of bodie and memorie overtake them, that they cannot sett any certeyne course or order therein (p. 11).

Statistics drawn from the 1560s show that at least 18 percent of all adults made wills; this number rose to only 19 percent by the 1620s. Most of the time the land of the deceased was divided among family and friends without any real authority or recourse: there was no legal requirement to make a will, although all people were considered capable of making valid wills unless they were declared disabled by law; were boys under fourteen years of age or girls under twelve; were convicted criminals (including suicides, recusants, or excommunicates); or were married women or mentally retarded.

When a woman married, any property she owned was legally transferred to her husband. With no property of her own to bequeath, she could make no will of her own, a convention bitterly contravened in the "Wyll and Testament" of Isabella Whitney.[16] She could, however, with her husband's permission, leave money given to her as an allowance during marriage, or goods she had purchased with such an allowance. She could also bequeath credits and legacies due to her if she possessed them at the time of her marriage. Between 1558 and 1639 less than a half percent of the testators were wives; and of these many were widows who had remarried. Widows remarrying could make freedom of testation a provision of their contract for a second marriage, especially when they had inherited from their former husband and wished to make bequests to the children of that earlier union. There were handbooks available for guidance—Henry Swinburne's *A Briefe Treatise of Testaments and Last Wills* (1590), the first standard English treatise to ecclesiastical probate procedures,[17] and Thomas Wentworth's *The Office and Duty of Executors*, as well as the formularies in the lengthy and detailed *Symbolaeographia ...; Or, The Notarie and Scrivener* (1590) collected by William West of the Inner Temple. Witnesses—at least two; perhaps three or four—had to attest to the will, although they did not need to be present when the will was drawn up. The use of marks rather than signatures was common.

Wills and testaments were not alike: wills disposed of real estate; testaments dealt with personal property such as goods or chattels—anything but land —although tenancies or leases could muddy the waters. Customarily, direct descendants were given preference over collateral relatives, men over women, the first-born son to the exclusion of later sons. It was, in fact, this practice that caused abrogation in most instances, when spouses, daughters, or younger sons were preferred: the stuff of controversy, and of dramatic plots. No family heirs were honored until all debts had first been paid. Then, traditionally in London (if not so often outside the city), half of the remaining property of a man was reserved for his wife or, if there were children, then one-third went to the widow, one-third to all of the children, and the final third, "the dead man's part," went to whoever or whatever the testator ascertained. A widow's claim on her husband's property could be dependent, however, on dowers or jointures, properties settled on the wife at marriage in order to entitle her to some part of the estate if her husband predeceased her. Sometimes the need to provide for spouses, daughters, and younger sons caused testators to override the practice of primogeniture and circumvent the laws and practices of inheritance that transferred land to the eldest son by making special provisions

Figure 15: Woodcut illustration showing the making of a will from "The Crie of the poore for the death of the Right Honorable Earle of Huntington" (1596)

as gifts or settlements before their deaths so long as the terms of their tenture permitted it.[18] Shakespeare's Lysander, looking for an inheritance from his widowed aunt, thinks of obtaining it while she is still alive. As he flees into the Athenian woods with Hermia in *A Midsummer Night's Dream*, he tells her,

I have a widow aunt, a dowager,
Of great revenue, and she hath no child.
From Athens is her house remote seven leagues;
And she respects me as her only son.
There, gentle Hermia, may I marry thee;
And to that place the sharp Athenian law
Cannot pursue us. If thou lovest me, then
Steal forth thy father's house to-morrow night;
And in the wood, a league without the town …
There will I stay for thee (1.1.157–68).

At the same time, Duke Theseus, equally impatient to wed the Amazon Hippolyta whom he conquered and brought to Athens from the New World, thinks otherwise:

> Now, fair Hippolyta, our nuptial hour
> Draws on apace. Four happy days bring in
> Another moon; but O, methinks, how slow
> This old moon [wanes]! She lingers my desires,
> Like to a step-dame, or a dowager,
> Long withering out a young man's revenue (1.1.1–6).

Ecclesiastical courts normally supervised the wills of widows and others, bolstered on occasion by bonds, accounts, and inventories, while common law courts handled cases of default or malpractice: "as early as 1530," Honigmann and Brock tell us, "it was advised that property should be dispersed before death to avoid the possibility of fraud after it" (p. 15).

Swinburne advises that "if a man should chance to be so wise, as to make his will in his good health, … that then surely he should not liue long after" (sig. F3). Honigmann and Brock note that, in their survey of playhouse wills, the average time between their writing and the testator's burial was two weeks, " a triumph," they sum, "of superstition over good sense" (p. 17). Normally, scribes wrote out wills from rough drafts or notes of the testator, leaving room for signatures of the author and his or her witnesses, and making corrections, emendations, and clarifications before the final draft was released. There were exceptions, of course. Honigmann and Brock found that "William Sly (1608) had no time to have his will drawn up formally before he died but he signed the rudimentary statement of his intentions which had been copied out and added a nuncupative codicil. John Underwood (1624) also added to his written bequests on his death-bed a few days after he had signed the fair copy and Edmund Tylney (1610) made provision in his will for 'What other legacies I shall give vppon my Death Bedd by Word of mouth'" (p. 18). Although written wills were by far the normal procedure, when death was swift or unexpected, goods—but not land—could be distributed by word of mouth.

Normally, the executor of a will arranged for the burial and then proved the document by taking it to the appropriate Church court—the archdeaconry court if the will dealt with goods and chattels exceeding £5 in value (known as *bona notabilia*) in a single archdeaconry, or a diocesan court, or a commissary court. Such courts protected this practice rigorously, and, say Honigmann and Brock, they "poach[ed] business where possible for the sake of the fees involved, especially in London where jursidictions overlapped both geographically and hierarchically." Furthermore, "[w]ith several courts close at hand" in London, "executors often elected to prove a will in the highest court for greater publicity and security of record" (p. 25). A certificate of probate, along with a copy of the will, was given to the executor; the original will, with the probate clause added and endorsed, was filed among court records and a copy was enrolled in the court registers. Generally, the deceased man's wife served as his executrix.[19] Monuments were not uncommon, but only those of higher rank could claim—as Shakespeare did—burial within the parish church rather than in the churchyard. To avoid the high cost of elaborate funerals, some (especially those of the aristocracy) were buried at night. The executor was responsible for burial expenses. He also paid off all the debts first, descending by rank of creditor.

A distraught Richard II would suspend such practices:

> Let's talk of graves, of worms, and epitaphs,
> Make dust our paper, and with rainy eyes
> Write sorrow on the bosom of the earth.
> Let's choose executors and talk of wills;
> And yet not so, for what can we bequeath
> Save our deposed bodies to the ground?
> Our lands, our lives, and all are Bullingbrook's,
> And nothing can we call our own but death,
> And that small model of the barren earth
> Which serves as paste and cover to our bones (*Richard II*, 3.2.
> 145–54),

but his self-pity is, cognitively, an exception. Rather, it is clear from compiled evidence that wills more normally "theorized … a set of customs produced by different attitudes to death and dying," as Lloyd Davis has it (p. 220) or, more generally and inclusively yet, wills strategized the meaning and significance of death by asserting the past, present or future agency and authority of the testator. Most commonly, as we have seen, there was the employment of charity—a dole of money or bread to the parish, money left to the poor, tokens and gifts for servants. But there were also far grander thoughts of facing death and living beyond it, suggesting yet more cognitive practices with wills. King Ferdinand of Navarre proposes to his three nobles Berowne, Longaville, and Dumaine, in *Love's Labor's Lost,* what all fear:

> grace us in the disgrace of death;
> When spite of cormorant devouring Time,
> Th' endeavor of this present breath may buy
> That honor which shall bate his scythe's keen edge,

And make us heirs of all eternity (1.1.3–7).

Margaret Spufford has suggested a key motive in making wills was "to provide for children who were not yet independent,"[20] such as Bertram and Helena; Lloyd Davis remarks that "This purpose influences the frequent naming of daughters, married or unmarried, as beneficiaries" and reconstructs some examples from Honigmann and Brock and from Amy Louise Erickson:

> Margaret Brayne left all belongings to her creditor Robert Myles, but charged him to "keepe, educate & bring vpp Katherine Brayne my husbandes daughter." … Jane Poley left a small annual amount to her eldest son, who may well, like many eldest sons, have received "preferential treatment by the common law of inheritance." … The large sum of £40 was given to her daughter Frauncis Wibard "for the maintenance of her and her poor children and the bringing up of them." … To her apparently childless second daughter, Anne Gibbes, Poley left a number of valued personal possessions, including "a hope ring of gold … her best petticoat guarded with velvet … one bolster which belongs to her bed." … Agnes Henslowe, the recent widow of theatre manager Philip, bequeathed money to a group of "eighty poor widows and women," with different amounts going to various other people and the "Rest to my only and well beloved daughter Joane Allen." … Elizabeth Cundall made the sharpest provision in her will, leaving her "goodes" to her daughter Elizabeth ffinch and £50 to her granddaughter Elizabeth Cundall. She then declared, "I doe intend the same as that my said sonne in lawe Mr herbert ffynch shall neuer haue possession of the same, … and I would have no parte of my estate neither prodigally spent, nor lewdly wasted by" her son, William Cundall (pp. 229–30).

Still, the simplest way to perpetuate one's self was to give offspring the same name.

Caring for those to follow was another way to strategize proceedings after death. Don Pedro tells Claudio that Hero is Leonato's only heir in *Much Ado about Nothing*, and when Claudio remarks of his interest in her—

O my lord,
When you went onward on this ended action,

I look'd upon her with a soldier's eye,
That lik'd, but had a rougher task in hand
Than to drive liking to the name of love.
But now I am return'd, and that war-thoughts
Have left their places vacant, in their rooms
Come thronging soft and delicate desires,
All prompting me how fair young Hero is,
Saying I lik'd her ere I went to wars (1.1.296–305)—

Don Pedro promises that he will perpetuate Leonato's lineage by supporting Claudio's interest in Hero: "If thou dost love fair Hero, cherish it, And I will break with her, and with her father, And thou shalt have her" (1.1.308–10). In securing the fortunes of lineage, inheritances can not only establish estates, but restore them, as Celia tells Rosalind in *As You Like It*: "You know my father hath no child but I, nor none is like to have; and truly when he dies, thou shalt be his heir; for what he hath taken away from thy father perforce, I will render thee again in affection. By mine honor, I will, and when I break that oath, let me turn monster" (1.2.17–22). A different kind of bequest, according to Davis, took the form of women's advice manuals (p. 232).

But bequests—including living bequests—could be distinctly political. This is what Octavius Caesar has in mind when he gives his sister Octavia to Antony:

There's my hand.
A sister I bequeath you, whom no brother
Did ever love so dearly. Let her live
To join our kingdoms and our hearts, and never
Fly off our loves again! (*Antony and Cleopatra*, 2.2.148–52).

But the plan backfires when Antony betrays him publicly; Antony, Octavius tells his sister,

hath wag'd
New wars 'gainst Pompey, made his will, and read it
To public ear;
Spake scantly of me; when perforce he could not
But pay me terms of honor, cold and sickly
He vented [them,] most narrow measure lent me;
When the best hint was given him, he not [took]'t,
Or did it from his teeth (3.4.3–10).

Antony learned in *Julius Caesar* how effective the public declamation of a will could be.

Wills could also function cognitively for more purely selfish reasons. The Duke of Milan uses the threat of disinheritance of his daughter Silvia in *The Two Gentlemen of Verona* to trick and test Valentine. He tells her suitor,

> trust me, she is peevish, sullen, froward,
> Proud, disobedient, stubborn, lacking duty,
> Neither regarding that she is my child,
> Nor fearing me as if I were her father;
> And may I say to thee, this pride of hers
> (Upon advice) hath drawn my love from her,
> And where I thought the remnant of mine age
> Should have been cherish'd by her child-like duty,
> I now am full resolv'd to take a wife,
> And turn her out to who will take her in:
> Then let her beauty be her wedding-dow'r,
> For me and my possessions she esteems not (3.1.68–79),

forecasting Lear's treatment of Cordelia (1.1.108–20; cf. Lear with Kent, 1.1.166–79). Iago is enraged because time in rank has not advanced him as he feels he deserves; "'Tis the curse of service; Preferment goes by letter and affection, And not by old gradation, where each second Stood heir to th' first" (*Othello*, 1.1.35–38). But it is most agonizingly, tragically, the aging Lear who, following the *Symbolaeographia* collected by William West, had thought to have planned his future out most carefully—

> Cornwall and Albany,
> With my daughter's dow'rs digest the third;
> Let pride, which she calls plainness, marry her.
> I do invest you jointly with my power,
> Pre-eminence, and all the large effects
> That troop with majesty. Ourself, by monthly course,
> With reservation of an hundred knights
> By you to be sustain'd, shall our abode
> Make with you by due turn. Only we shall retain
> The name, and all th' addition to a king;
> The sway, revenue, execution of the rest,
> Beloved sons, be yours, which to confirm,
> This coronet part between you (1.1.127–39)—

following Part I, Book 2, section 424 of the *First Part* of *Symbolaeographia* to the letter. West had written,

> A gift of goods and chattels, with couenants to find the donors necessaries, and performe his will [gives all the donor's] leasses, farmes, and termes of yeares, cattels, implements, houshold-stuffe, beasts and cattell, and all his other goods, as well reall as personall, moueable as vnmoueable whatsoeuer. … In consideration whereof [the recipient of the gift covenants that he and his executors] shall and will find and prouide to the said R. [the donor] during his naturall life, conuenient and sufficient meat, drink, and apparell, And also one comely and decent Parlor or chamber for the said R., to lie in seuerally, with fire and candle necessarie, during his naturall lyfe, and one person to attend vpon him during the time aforesaid,[21]

only royally extending the single servant into "an hundred knights," so that Goneril feels justified in reducing the number to fifty (1.4.293) and Regan further reduces the number to twenty-five (2.4.248) before going beyond even West, asking, "What need one?" (2.4.263).

But hedging against the future took place not only on the stage of the Globe, at court, or in the great halls of manor houses where *King Lear* was performed, but also nearer to home, in Stratford-upon-Avon, Warwickshire. There was, for instance, the case of Robert Perrott, a rich brewer, who leased the tavern called King's Hall or King's House in Rother Street near the White Swan. "His characteristically Puritan will," Mark Eccles remarks,

> left Luscombe manor in Snitterfield to his grandson Ezechias Woodward, who had studied at Oxford, and gave money for the poor, for the preacher of a yearly sermon, and for the corporation "to make merye withall after the sermon is ended." His example in endowing a yearly sermon [perpetually in his name] was later followed by Hamlet Smith and by Shakespeare's friends John and Thomas Combe.[22]

Shakespeare's will also scripts the future long after the playwright's death. The Stratford antiquarian Joseph Greene was the first person to turn up a transcript of Shakespeare's testament, in 1747, and was dismayed by what he found. "The Legacies and Bequests therein," he remarks, "are undoubtedly as he intended; but the manner of introducing them, appears to me so dull and irregular, so absolutely void of ye least particle of that Spirit which Animated Our great Poet; that it must lessen his Character as a Writer, to imagine ye least Sentence of it his production."[23] Park Honan agrees, arguing that "Shakespeare reminds one of the Duke in *Measure for Measure*, hoping to control a story that has gone out of line."

> "Item. I give and bequeath unto my son-in-l[aw]—hearing those words or copying them from the early draft, his lawyer stopped and changed "son-in-law" to read "daughter Judyth." Quiney [her husband] is humiliated by not being mentioned. Other relatives by marriage, too, are ignored. … Shakespeare is fairly hard even on Judith [his younger daughter] to whom he leaves £150—far less than he gives to her richer sister [Susanna]—and conditions are attached even to Judith's main sum. She is allowed £100 as a marriage portion, but the remaining £50 will be hers only if she renounces a claim to a "copyhold tenement," or the cottage on Chapel Lane. Judith is left a further £150 if she, or any issue of her body, be living after three years, the annual interest earned, not the principal, will then go to her issue, or to Judith if she is still married. Any "such husbond" as she then has will be able to claim the sum only on condition that he settles on his wife lands worth £150. … What is unusual is the urgent extent to which Shakespeare goes in order to guide his estate into the far future. He grants land in tail male, to forestall a division of property in future between daughters and wives, and the main legatee Susanna Hall [his elder married daughter] is left nearly everything. Here, he is as generous as Lear is at first with Goneril—
>
> All my barns, stables, orchards, gardens, lands, tenements & hereditaments whatsoever, situate, lying and being or to be had … within the towns and hamlets, villages, fields & grounds of Stratford upon Avon, Old Stratford, Bishopton & Welcombe …

All of that, including New Place [his large home in Stratford], the Henley Street tenements and London's Blackfriars gatehouse are to be Susanna's "to have and to hold."

But he is intent on enumerating her non-existing heirs, who are seen as young males to be born from as yet unborn male bodies (pp. 395–96). Shakespeare's most famous remark—"Item. I gyve unto my wief my second best bed with the furniture"—valence, linens, and hangings—has been variously interpreted, but according to David Harris Sacks, it was a convention in wills of this time that a person's heir

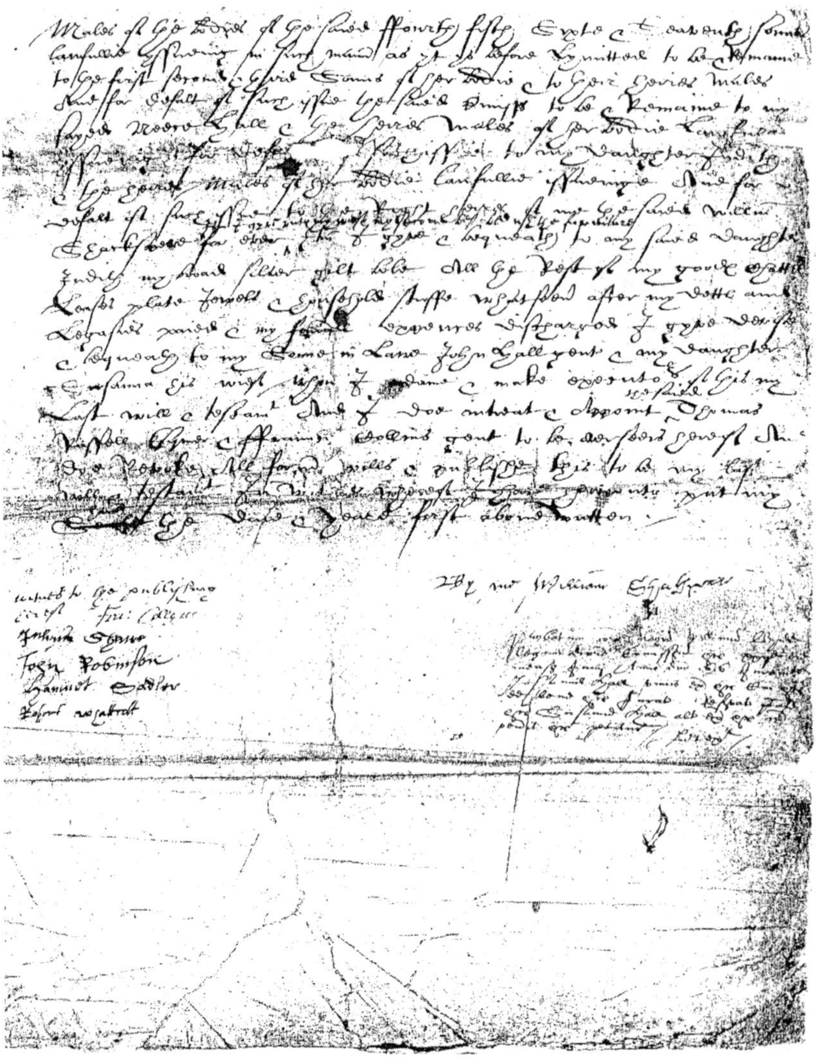

Figure 16: The third and final page of Shakespeare's will with his signature

received the best bed—Susanna in this case—and that the wife received the second best one.[24] To others, Shakespeare leaves articles of clothing, plate, a sword, memorial rings for his fellow sharers and players, and money for his godson William Walker and the poor of Stratford. It is all very complicated in its detail, especially alongside such a document as the last implied will in Shakespeare's plays—Prospero's in *The Tempest*. "I'll break my staff," Prospero says, "Bury it certain fadoms in the earth, And deeper than did ever plummet sound I'll drown my book" (5.1.54–57); in addition, he acknowledges Caliban (5.1.275–76) and leaves the dukedom of Milan to Ferdinand and Miranda (5.1.308–11) so that "Every third thought shall be my grave" (5.1.312). In *All's Well That Ends Well* there is no indication that Bertram's father, unlike Helena's, left any will with specific provisions.

Because of a testator's composition of a will and the executor's subsequent actions, wills are both private and public documents. They may be personal, but they cannot remain altogether secret. Cognitively, then, in Shakespeare as in his larger culture, the peculiar flexibility or indeterminacy of wills meant they could favor, inhibit, restrict, punish, instruct, cheat, empower, protect, confine, enlighten, demoralize, politicize, betray, or encourage. This is Bertram's particular humiliation; his father died before he reached majority, and everyone knows he is left impoverished for the time being and at the mercy of the King of France: "I … weep o'er my father's death anew; but I must attend his Majesty's command, to whom I am now in ward, evermore in subjection" (1.1.3–5). The strikingly inaccurate *evermore* reveals his state of mind over his state of disinheritance. All is openly at sixes and sevens. There is nothing that can be done about it. But initially, Helena is no better off. Once the Countess has discovered her best-kept secret—her love for the socially unavailable Bertram—the Countess must evaluate her new awareness: "Speak, is't so? If it be so, you have wound a goodly clew" (1.3.181–82), a proverbial expression for an impossible situation. Wards like Bertram traditionally went into military service; "I'll to the Tuscan wars, and never bed her," he says (2.3.273; cf. 296). Adopted daughters like Helena, whose situation is similar to that of a ward except that she has control of her inheritance, the decisive and vital medical knowledge, often went into the convent, and she makes her way in a pilgrim's habit to Saint Jaques le Grand. Both Bertram and Helena initially make conventional gestures of response. But the web of their experiences, together as youth before the play starts and separately in coming of age as the play progresses, leads to another related image that the First Lord observes: "The web of our life," he contends more universally, "is of a mingled yarn, good and ill together: our virtues would be proud, if our faults whipt them not, and our crimes would despair, if they were not cherish'd by our virtues" (4.3.71–74).

Lives, like wills, can unwind in complicated ways, but when they incorporate "good and ill together," when they teach the tempering of pride—what both the ambitious Helena and the obdurate Bertram must learn at some cost—and when they lead to a despair that must be controlled—as Bertram and Helena both feel for quite different reasons at their initial separation in 1.1.—they learn to accept each other as equals, even if it is as tentative as the conditional acceptance of Helena by Bertram at the play's end. The wills drawn up by the dead need to join with the wills of those still living. In the case of *All's Well That Ends Well*, the wills of the four main characters realize the written wills we never see, but cognitively reconceived through the actions of both parties, lead to the comic ending toward which the play has been moving all along.

SHAKESPEARE'S LEGACY

In one swift act of cognition, moving from a particular act to its universal significance, from drama to metadrama, Cassius invites his fellow assassins of Julius Caesar to "Stoop, then, and wash," echoing Brutus' earlier command to "Stoop, Romans, stoop, And let us bathe our hands in Caesar's blood," and then makes a pronouncement that leaps at once out of the play's chronology:

> How many ages hence
> Shall this our lofty scene be acted over
> In [states] unborn and accents yet unknown! (*Julius Caesar*, 3.1.105; 111–13).

But Brutus would hold on to his superior authority by displacing such a thought:

> How many times shall Caesar bleed in sport,
> That now on Pompey's basis [lies] along
> No worthier than the dust! (3.1.114–16)

These differing, and at base contentious, perspectives demonstrate how the brain does not just see, hear, or feel the outside world, but rather constructs its own interpretive and regulating response to the world's stimuli. Those outside stimuli, what we have called lightwaves striking the eye's retina, are hastened along the optic nerve and taken along neural pathways to the cerebral cortex to establish and order meanings. But the meanings that result, as we have seen repeatedly in this book, depend as much on previous neural associations as current or new ones; the worn pathways and synapses suggest that any cognitive response is in large part unconscious, drawing on the predispositions of a person's past and a person's culture. Cognition is not, finally, what we see but what we think; and not about a single matter (although that may be the stimulus, as the blood of Caesar here surely is) but a complex accumulation of matters brought together in the convergence zone of the cerebral cortex, issuing forth as mistakenly perceived conscious thoughts of the moment. Caesar's death may be continually reenacted—may have to be continually reenacted—to ensure human liberty in the way Cassius conceives it; and it must be continually reenacted for Shakespeare to make his living.

Drama as Shakespeare contrived it lived in performance, not in publication; and, as such, it continually stimulated, and relied on, the cognition of spectators. On a virtually bare stage, Shakespeare's collaborators were not only his fellow players but the playgoers, who had always to provide reactions to what was both seen on the stage and what was referred to but not necessarily seen there. Cognitive responses to a play could always be seeded, but their outcome was not certain. Sir Walter Ralegh, among others of Shakespeare's contemporaries, comments on such indeterminacy. The internal working of his fellow men, he noted, was remote, indecipherable, even inaccessible: "I may tell what the outward object seemeth to me, but what it seemeth to other creatures, or whether it be indeed that which it seemeth to me, or any other of them, I know not."[1] Learning the thoughts of others in response to a historic event such as an assassination may seem unnecessary but it is unavailable; and such thoughts, as we have seen, may themselves change. "The brain-mind's continual struggle to categorize sensory phenomena—an elusive collection of oscillating excitatory patterns," writes Barbara Maria Stafford, "nicely corresponds to the distributed view of cognition recently proposed by Andy Clark. According to this cognitive scientist, the 'extended mind' enlists objects that are scattered throughout the ambient to shape its neurological systems by 'intertwining sensing with acting and moving in the world.'"[2]

Brutus himself is restless through much of *Julius Caesar*, and the appearance of Caesar's ghost to him on the eve of the battle at Philippi suggests that his restlessness has far from ended with Caesar's death. Antony and Cassius change as well; and their actions suggest that recognition continually takes place as events in Roman history unfold. Their thoughts are combinatoric, like those of Othello or Iago, Lear or Leontes are, in Rebecca Goldstein's term,[3] because certain stimuli are under constant neural rearrangement and change as they attempt to collect new reactions for different or modified associations. "The necessary incompleteness of even our formal systems of thought demonstrates that there is no non-shifting foundation on which any system rests. All truths—even those that had seemed so certain as to be immune to the very possibility of revision—are essentially manufactured. Indeed, the very notion of the objectively true is a socially constructed myth. Rather the entire notion of truth is embedded in our minds, which are themselves the unwitting lackeys of organizational forms of influence" (p. 25).[4]

Drama relies on conscious perception, understanding, and interpretation of events and the recognizable objects, the visible and invisible stage properties, on which they are initiated and grounded, are seen, directly or in the mind's eye. Indeed, scientists have now found the eye to be one of the strongest parts of the human organism. "Although people may think of their body as a fairly permanent structure," writes Nicholas Wade, "most of it is in a state of constant flux as old cells are discarded and new ones are generated in their place. Each kind of tissue [like established neural pathways] has its own turnover time. But the lens cells of the eye, neurons of the cerebral cortex … last a lifetime."[5] Images are momentary, as Aristotle recognized, succeeded by other images. Cognitively focusing on perceptions and processing them results in what Aristotle terms knowledge—that which man cannot live without—and is the primary job of intellect.

But we perceive only what is given us to work with; that is what Shakespeare knew so well. We cannot perceive, understand, or hope to know Shylock fully without taking into account the ring that Leah gave him as a bachelor and what it means to him. Perception is never entirely free; it must begin with some stimulus; that too Aristotle and Shakespeare both knew. Consciousness can never overcome the limitations of vision. Sight remains fundamental both to Aristotle and Shakespeare. But objects and events outside the brain are without meaning unless they prompt neural patterns by which the brain creates a reality of significance rather than accept a passive mirror image that merely gives back what it took in. "Individual shapes—like single neurons firing—must cross, not rise to, a certain threshold of intensity to meld into conscious unity," Stafford contends. She continues,

> To achieve this lateral linkage adding up to a continuous experience of immediacy, groups of neurons as well as groups of ornament must ally themselves with other parts of the brain … to constitute a coalition. … The distribution of minute and repetitive elements causes the viewer to vacillate between seeing scatter or blend. The perception of coherence is always hard-won, the result of the ephemeral framing of a wealth of overlapping detail. Art consists not just in crossing the threshold of intensity that comes from transforming the many into one, but in holding our attention there. Perhaps consciousness is definable, after all, as just this persistence of an intensified collection of perceptions that outlasts any particular stimulus (pp. 334–35).

It is, in the final analysis, the collocation of perceptions that Shakespeare's plays stimulate that causes them to play in states unborn and accents still unknown. Shakespeare's legacy is that he seizes upon the complexity of thought, of objects seen and imagined, as they are processed by a brain that already has certain well-worn genetic, experiential, and cultural responses, and, making use of their essential plurisignificance and ambiguity—what John Carey identifies as an "idea-bank" that results in participatory "indistinctness,"[6]—writes his plays in such a way that certain key moments have potentially conflicted meanings, that there is only indeterminacy at the heart of the most lasting drama. Thus, his plays, like those of his fellow playwrights, focus in part on those objects that give rise to personal, public, and cultural meanings that ensure widespread if ultimately unsettled and incomplete knowledge. That keeps Shakespeare's plays alive. And it keeps Aristotelian man alive, too, yearning to know.

NOTES

PREFACE

1. All references to Shakespeare in this study are to the Riverside edition of Shakespeare's plays, Eds. G. Blakemore Evans, Harry Levin, Herschel Baker, Anne Barton, Frank Kermode, Hallett Smith and Marie Edel (Boston: Houghton Mifflin Company, 1974).
2. These examples are drawn from *Staged Properties in Early Modern English Drama*, Eds. Jonathan Gil Harris and Natasha Korda (Cambridge: Cambridge University Press, 2002), p. 3.
3. James Calderwood, *Shakespearean Metadrama* (Minneapolis: University of Minnesota Press, 1971), p. 13.
4. E.K. Chambers, *The Elizabethan Stage*, 4 vols. (Oxford: Clarendon Press, 1923), I, 352.
5. Thomas Heywood, *An Apology for Actors* (London: The Shakespeare Society, 1841), p. 51.
6. John J. Ratney, *A User's Guide to the Brain* (New York: Random House Vintage Books, 2002), p. 199.
7. In an email from Paul Marquis October 21, 2004.
8. Rita Carter, *Mapping the Mind* (Berkeley: University of California Press, 1999), p. 131.
9. Edward Said, cited by Yu Jin Ko, *Mutability and Divison on Shakespeare's Stage* (Newark: University of Delaware Press, 2004), p. 7.
10. Jacques Derrida, cited in Davide Del Bello, *Forgotten Paths*, an unpublished MS, p. 182.

ARISTOTLE'S LEGACY

1. Aristotle, *Metaphysics*, trans. W.D. Ross in *The Basic Works of Aristotle*, Ed. Richard McKeon (New York: Random House, 1941), p. 689.
2. Aristotle, *Posterior Analytics* II.19, tr. G.R.G. Moore in McKeon, p. 185.
3. Aristotle, *De Anima*, II.7, trans. J.A. Smith in McKeon, p. 583.
4. St. Thomas Aquinas, *Basic Writings*, Ed. Anton C. Pegis. 2 vols. New York: Random House, 1944), p. 739.
5. Robert Pasnau, *Theories of Cognition in the Later Middle Ages* (Cambridge: Cambridge University Press, 1997), pp. 254, 257.
6. *The Notebooks of Leonardo de Vinci*, Ed. Edward MacCurdy. 2 vols. (London: The Reprint Society, 1938, 1954), I, 208.
7. Nicholas Humphrey, *A History of the Mind* (New York: Simon and Schuster, 1992), p. 52.
8. James Shapiro, *A Year in the Life of William Shakespeare: 1599* (New York: Harper Collins, 2005), p. 25.
9. Shapiro, p. 8
10. Frederick Kiefer, *Shakespeare's Visual Theatre: Staging the Personified Characters* (Cambridge: Cambridge University Press, 2003), pp. 9–10.
11. This was exaggerated by the sudden increase in luxury goods imported from 1507 onward. See Linda Levy Peck, *Consuming Splendor* (Cambridge: Cambridge University Press, 2005), pp. 16, 19, 27, 31–33, 45, 69–70.
12. Quoted by Katharine Eisaman Maus in *Inwardness and Theater in the English Renaissance* (Chicago: University of Chicago Press, 1995), p. 99.
13. David Riggs, *The World of Christopher Marlowe* (London: Faber and Faber, 2004), pp. 228–29.
14. Geoffrey Tillotson, *Times Literary Supplement*, 20 July, 1933, p. 494.
15. Ruth Lunney, *Marlowe and the Popular Tradition: Innovations in the English Drama before 1595* (Manchester: Manchester University Press, 2002), p. 44.
16. Quoted by Tiffany Stern in *Making Shakespeare: From Stage to Page* (London: Routledge, 2004), p. 98. In *La Bete delle Immagini*, Lina Bolzoni argues that the use of the mind's eye was invoked by medieval Dominicans. Ingrid Rowland summarizes the argument this way: "Dominicans used vernacular language, and, as Bolzoni shows at length, they used pictures, not only the magnificent paintings that decorated their churches and convents, but also the pictures that listeners were asked to conjure up in their minds. Their aim was not simply to move congregations during a sermon, but to teach, to make the sermon memorable. The more vivid the images, the more musical the words, the more likely that their underlying message would also stay fixed in place long after the sermon was over." Rowland's comments appear in *The New York Review of Books* 52:16 (October 20, 2005) p.35.

17. Christopher Marlowe, *Dido, Queen of Carthage*, in *The Complete Plays*, Ed. Mark Thornton Burnett (London: J.M. Dent Everyman, 1999), 2.1.193–99.
18. Tør Norretranders, *The User Illusion: Cutting Consciousness Down to Size*, trans. Jonathan Sydenham (New York: Penguin Books, 1998), p. 186.
19. Paul M. Matthews and Jeffrey McQuain, *The Bard on the Brain* (New York: The Dana Press, 2003), p. 44.
20. The observations in this paragraph are drawn from Michael S. Gazzaniga, *The Mind's Past* (Berkeley: University of California Press, 1998), p. 86, and Steven Pinker, *How the Mind Works* (New York: W.W. Norton and Co., 1997), pp. 257, 243.
21. This material is drawn from John J. Ratney, *A User's Guide to the Brain* (New York: Random House Vintage Books. 2002), pp. 99–101; Gazzaniga, pp. 74, 36; and John J. Dowling, *Creating Mind: How the Brain Works* (New York: W.W. Norton and Co., 1998), pp. 113–17.
22. Harold Love, *Attributing Authorship: An Introduction* (Cambridge: Cambridge University Press, 2002), p. 4.
23. Samuel Daniel, *Selected Poetry and "A Defense of Rhyme,"* Eds. Geoffrey G. Hiller and Peter L. Groves (Asheville, NC: Pegasus, 1998), p. 206.
24. V.S. Ramachandran and Sandra Blakeslee, *Phantoms in the Brain* (New York: HarperCollins edition, 1999), p. 89.
25. Rita Carter, *Mapping the Mind* (Berkeley: University of California Press, 1999), p. 108.
26. Gazzaniga, pp. 63–64.
27. Aristotle, *Posterior Analytics*, trans. A.J. Jenkinson, in McKeon, p. 185.
28. Aristotle, *De Sensu* and *De Memoria*, trans. G.R.T. Rose (Cambridge: Cambridge University Press, 1906), p. 103.
29. John C. Meagher, *Pursuing Shakespeare's Dramaturgy: Some Contexts, Resources, and Strategies in His Playmaking* (Madison, NJ: Fairleigh Dickinson University Press, 2003), p. 289.

SHAKESPEARE'S CROWNS

1. Marjorie Garber, *Shakespeare After All* (New York: Pantheon, 2004), p. 414.
2. My text is the 1631 edition printed by George Miller and sold at the sign of the Black Bear in Paul's Churchyard.
3. Ernest Schanzer, *The Problem Plays of Shakespeare* (London: Routledge and Kegan Paul, 1963), p. 11.
4. Thomas Heywood, *Apology for Actors*, quoted in John Drakakis, "'Fashion it thus': Julius Caesar and the Politics of Theatrical Representation," in *New Casebooks: Julius Caesar*, Ed. Richard Wilson (Houndsmills, Basingstoke: Palgrave, 2002), p. 78.

5. My text for *Tamburlaine I* is that in *English Renaissance Drama*, Eds. David Bevington, Lars Engle, Katharine Eisaman Maus, and Eric Rasmussen (New York: W.W. Norton and Co., 2002).
6. *Workes* (1616), sig. P6v.
7. John N. King, *Tudor Royal Iconography: Literature and Art in an Age of Religious Crisis* (Princeton: Princeton University Press, 1989), p. 227.
8. Richard Mulcaster, The *Queens Maiesties Passage* (1559), sigs. D3v-D4.
9. Mulcaster, sigs. C3v-C4.
10. Quoted by King, p. 228.
11. My text for Christopher Marlowe, *The Troublesome Reign and Lamentable Death of Edward the Second* is that in *Renaissance Drama: An Anthology of Plays and Entertainments*, Ed. Arthur F. Kinney second ed. (Oxford: Blackwell Publishing, 2005).
12. My text for W.S., *The Lamentable Tragedie of Locrine* is that in *The Shakespeare Apocrypha,* Ed. C.F. Tucker Brooke (Oxford: Clarendon Press, 1908; 1967).
13. My text for the anonymous *Raigne of King Edward the Third* is that in *The Shakespeare Apocrypha* Ed. C.F. Tucker Brooke.
14. My text for Christopher Marlowe, *The Massacre at Paris,* is that in *The Complete Plays*, Ed. Mark Thornton Burnett (London: J.M. Dent Everyman, 1999).
15. Andrew Gurr, "Headgear as a Paralinguistic Signifier in *King Lear*," *Shakespeare Survey* 55 (2002), pp. 50–51.
16. George Buchanan (1689 edition in English, p. 13) as quoted by James Emerson Phillips, "The Monarchic Cycle in *Julius Caesar* and *Antony and Cleopatra*," in *Shakespeare's Julius Caesar*, Ed. Julian Markels (New York: Charles Scribner's Sons, 1961), p. 91.
17. My text for Christopher Marlowe's *The Jew of Malta* is the Revels Student Edition, Ed. David Bevington (Manchester: Manchester University Press, 1997).
18. Jenny Wormald in *Scots and Britons*, Ed. Roger A. Mason (Cambridge: Cambridge University Press, 1994), p. 22.
19. Quoted by Carole Levin in "*The Heart and Stomach of a King*": *Elizabeth I and the Politics of Sex and Power* (Philadelphia: University of Pennsylvania Press, 1994), p. 7.
20. Stephen Orgel, *The Authentic Shakespeare: And Other Problems of the Early Modern Stage* (London: Routledge, 2002), p. 127.
21. Wormald in *Scots and Britons*, Ed. Roger A. Mason, p. 19.
22. John Nichols, *The Progresses, Processions, and Magnificent Festivities of King James the First, His Royal Consort, Family, and Court*. 4 vols. (London: Society of Antiquaries, 1828), I, 49.
23. *Henslowe's Diary*, Eds. R.A. Foakes and R.T. Rickert (Cambridge: Cambridge University Press, 1968), Appendix 2, pp. 320–21.

24. Ernst H. Kantorowicz, *The King's Two Bodies: A Study in Medieval Political Theology* (Princeton: Princeton University Press, 1957), p. 496.
25. The material on Rogers, Aske, and Lloyd is taken from King, pp. 242–43.
26. Quoted by King as an epigraph on p. 116.
27. Quoted by Allan H. Gilbert, "The Wreath of Thorns in *Paradise Regained*," *Journal of the Warburg and Courtauld Institutes*, 3:1/2 (October 1939-January 1940), p. 157.
28. Quoted by Gilbert, p. 159.

SHAKESPEARE'S RINGS

1. Charles J. Fillmore, "Frame Semantics and the Nature of Language," *Annals of the New York Academy of Sciences: Conference on the Origin and Development of Language and Speech* 280 (1976), pp. 20–32.
2. John J. Ratney, *A User's Guide to the Brain* (New York: Random House Vintage Books, 2002), p. 174.
3. My text is that in *Renaissance Drama: An Anthology of Plays and Entertainments*, Ed. Arthur F. Kinney, second ed. (Oxford: Blackwell Publishing, 2005).
4. *Playhouse Wills 1558-1642*, Eds. E.A.J. Honigmann and Susan Brock (Manchester: Manchester University Press, 1993), p. 108.
5. Honigmann and Brock, p. 58.
6. Honigmann and Brock, p. 147.
7. Honigmann and Brock, p. 151.
8. Honigmann and Brock, p. 212.
9. The Massinger text is that in *English Renaissance Drama*, Eds. David Bevington, Lars Engle, Katharine Eisaman Maus, and Eric Rasmussen (New York: W.W. Norton and Co., 2002).
10. My text is that in *The Routledge Anthology of Renaissance Drama*, Ed. Simon Barker and Hilary Hinds (London: Routledge, 2003).
11. Quoted by Ronald M. Berger, *The Most Necessary Luxuries: The Mercers' Company of Coventry, 1550-1680* (University Park: Pennsylvania State University Press, 1993), p. 29.
12. Quoted by Charles Edelman in his edition of *The Merchant of Venice* (Cambridge: Cambridge University Press, 2002), p. 182.
13. David Cressy, *Birth, Marriage, and Death: Ritual, Religion, and the Life-Cycle in Tudor and Stuart England* (Oxford: Oxford University Press, 1997), pp. 233–34.
14. Quoted by Cressy, p. 263.
15. Cressy, p. 264.
16. The material on betrothings is taken largely from Cressy, ch. 11.
17. My text for Marlowe's *Jew of Malta* is the Revels edition, Ed. David Bevington (Manchester: Manchester University Press, 1997).

18. I am citing here B.J. Sokol and Mary Sokol, *Shakespeare, Law and Marriage* (Cambridge: Cambridge University Press, 2003), p. 81.
19. My text is from *Shakespeare's "Measure for Measure,"* Eds. Ivo Kamps and Karen Raber (Boston: Bedford/St. Martin's Press, 2004), pp. 218–19.
20. *Sarum Missal in English*, trans. Warren quoted by Cressy, p. 342; Sir Thomas Browne, *Pseudodoxia Epidemica: or, Enquiries into Very Many Received Tenets and Commonly Presumed Truths*, second ed. (1650), pp. 157–58.
21. J. Cordy Jefferson in *Brides and Bridals* (1872) quoted by Leonard R. N. Ashley, *Elizabethan Popular Culture* (Bowling Green, OH: Bowling Green State University Popular Press, 1988), p. 197.
22. Matthew Griffith, *Bethel: Or, a Forme for Families* (1633), p. 292.
23. Henry Smith, *A Preparative to Marriage* (1591), p. 24.
24. Ashley, p. 128.
25. Quoted by Cressy, p. 343.
26. These instances are drawn from Cressy, pp. 343–44.
27. Sokol and Sokol, pp. 91–92; 113–14.
28. Sokol and Sokol, p. 88.
29. Joan Evans, *English Posies and Posy Rings* (London: Oxford University Press, 1931), p. xi.
30. Herbert Norris, *Tudor Costume and Fashion* (Mineola, NY: Dover Publications, Inc., 1997), p. 359.
31. Quoted by Norris, p. 463.
32. Quoted by Norris, p. 463.
33. The material on posies is taken from Norris, pp. xi–xxiv.
34. Quoted by Jackson Campbell Boswell, "Shylock's Turquoise Ring," *Shakespeare Quarterly* 14:4 (Autumns 1963), p. 481.
35. Boswell, p. 481.
36. Boswell, p. 482.
37. Boswell, p. 482.
38. My text is that in Barker and Hinds.
39. Quoted by Boswell, p. 482.
40. Quoted by Boswell, p. 482.
41. Honigmann and Brock, p. 40.
42. Honigmann and Brock, p. 121.
43. Honigmann and Brock, p. 191.
44. Quoted by Cressy, p. 442.
45. Quoted by Cressy, p. 442.
46. Honigmann and Brock, p. 8.
47. Honigmann and Brock, p. 66.
48. Park Honan, *Shakespeare: A Life* (Oxford: Oxford University Press, 1998), p. 341; Honigmann and Brock, p. 107.

49. Marjorie Garber, *Shakespeare After All* (New York: Pantheon, 2004), p. 307.
50. My text for Middleton and Rowley's *The Changeling* is that in Kinney.
51. My text for Fletcher's *The Woman's Prize or The Tamer Tamed* is that in Bevington et al.

SHAKESPEARE'S BELLS

1. John Turner, *Macbeth* (Buckingham: Open University, 1992), p. 77.
2. My text is that in *The Shakespeare Apocrypha*, Ed. C.F. Tucker Brooke (Oxford: Clarendon Press, 1908; 1967).
3. These examples are taken from Alan C. Dessen and Leslie Thomson, *A Dictionary of Stage Directions in English Drama, 1580-1642* (Cambridge: Cambridge University Press, 1999), p. 28.
4. Dessen and Thomson, p. 28.
5. Peter Ackroyd, *Shakespeare the Biography* (New York: Nan A. Talese Doubleday. 2005), pp. 348–49.
6. Bruce R. Smith, *The Acoustic World of Early Modern England* (Chicago: University of Chicago Press, 1999), p. 219. He adds that "David Munrow describes a chime as something more like a set of miniature cymbals: hung in a wood frame, the hemisphere-shaped chimes were struck with hammers, not rung by hand" (pp. 219–20).
7. My text for *The Roaring Girl* is that in The *Routledge Anthology of Renaissance Drama*, Eds. Simon Barker and Hilary Hinds (London: Routledge, 2003).
8. David Cressy, *Bonfires and Bells: National Memory and the Protestant Calendar in Elizabethan and Stuart England* (Berkeley: University of California Press, 1989), p. 67.
9. My text is that in *The Shakespeare Apocrypha*, Ed. Tucker Brooke.
10. My text is that in *Renaissance Drama: An Anthology of Plays and Entertainments*, Ed. Arthur F. Kinney, second ed. (Oxford: Blackwell Publishing, 2005).
11. Smith's source is John Stow, *A Survey of London*, 2 vols., Ed. Charles Lethbridge Kingsford (Oxford: Clarendon Press, 1971), I:254, 256.
12. Quoted by Wes Folkerth, *The Sound of Shakespeare* (London: Routledge, 2002), p. 63.
13. My text is that in Barker and Hinds.
14. Eamon Duffy, *The Stripping of the Altars: Traditional Religion in England c. 1400-1580* (New Haven: Yale University Press, 1992), p. 126.
15. James Shapiro, *A Year in the Life of William Shakespeare: 1599* (New York: Harper Collins, 2005), p.166.
16. Cressy, pp. 50–58; cf. Liza Picard, *Elizabeth's London: Everyday Life in Elizabethan London* (New York: St. Martin's Press, 2003), p. 12.
17. Cressy, p. 72.

18. My text for Anthony Munday and others, *Sir Thomas More*, Eds. Vittorio Gabrieli and Giorgio Melchiori (Manchester: Manchester University Press, 1990).
19. David Cressy, *Birth, Marriage, and Death: Ritual, Religion, and the Life-Cycle in Tudor and Stuart England* (Oxford: Oxford University Press, 1997), p. 421.
20. Cressy, *Birth*, p. 422.
21. Cressy, *Birth*, p. 422.
22. Cressy, *Birth*, p. 423.
23. Cressy, *Birth*, p. 423.
24. Quoted by Cressy, *Birth*, p. 423.
25. Quoted by Cressy, *Birth*, p. 423.
26. Quoted by Cressy, *Birth*, p. 423.
27. Quoted by Cressy, *Birth*, p. 424.
28. Quoted by Cressy, *Birth*, p. 424.
29. Cressy, *Birth*, p. 425.
30. Reprinted in *London in the Age of Shakespeare: An Anthology*, Ed. Lawrence Manley (University Park: Pennsylvania State University Press, 1986), p. 41.
31. My text for The *Revenger's Tragedy* is that in *English Renaissance Drama*, Eds. David Bevington, Lars Engle, Katharine Eisman Maus, and Eric Rasmussen (New York: W.W. Norton and Co., 2002).
32. My text for Christopher Marlowe's *The Jew of Malta*, Ed. David Bevington (Manchester: Manchester University Press, 1997).
33. The material in this paragraph is drawn from Picard, pp. 188–89.
34. Duffy, p. 359.
35. Quoted by Park Honan, *Shakespeare: A Life* (Oxford: Oxford University Press, 1998), p. 230.
36. My text for *Volpone*, Eds. Bevington et al.
37. My text is Thomas Nashe, The *Unfortunate Traveller*, Ed. Paul Salzman (Oxford: Oxford University Press, 1998).
38. Quoted by F.P. Wilson, *The Plague in Shakespeare's London* (Oxford: Oxford University Press, 1927, 1963). p. 61. Other material on the plague in the following pages has been drawn from Wilson, pp. 3–128.
39. Thomas Dekker, *The Seven Deadly Sinnes* (1606), sig. Glv.
40. Dekker, quoted by Wilson, p. 97.
41. Picard, p. 90. She quotes Phaire on p. 91.
42. My text for John Webster's *The White Devil*, Eds. Bevington et al.
43. Geoffrey Bullough, *Narrative and Dramatic Sources of Shakespeare*, 8 vols. (New York: Columbia University Press, 1973), VII, 445–46. His quotation of *Illustris Viri* is from the trans. in *Popish Politics and Practice* (anonymous, 1674), pp. 28–31.
44. Quoted by Folkerth, p. 13.

SHAKESPEARE'S WILLS

1. B.J. Sokol and Mary Sokol, *Shakespeare, Law, and Marriage* (Cambridge: Cambridge University Press, 2003), pp. 43–44.
2. Lawrence Stone, *The Crisis of the Aristocracy, 1558-1641* (Oxford: Clarendon Press, l965), pp. 602, 601.
3. Quoted by Stone, p. 604.
4. Luke Wilson, *Theaters of Intention: Drama and the Law in Early Modern England* (Stanford: Stanford University Press, 2000), pp. 131–32; 133.
5. Natasha Korda, *Shakespeare's Domestic Economies: Gender and Property in Early Modern England* (Philadelphia: University of Pennsylvania Press, 2002), pp. 42–43.
6. Sheldon P. Zitner, *All's Well That Ends Well* (Boston: Twayne Publishers, 1989), p. 47.
7. Lloyd Davis, "Women's Wills in Early Modern England" in *Women, Property, and the Letters of the Law in Early Modern England*, Eds. Nancy E. Wright, Margaret W. Ferguson, and A.R. Buck (Toronto: University of Toronto Press, 2004), p. 223.
8. The text of George Chapman, *The Widow's Tears* is that ed. Akihiro Yamada for the Revels ed. (London: Methuen, 1975). See Davis for a discussion of this play and of Thomas Heywood, *A Fair Maid of the West* (c. 1603; published 1631).
9. My text for *The Pvritaine* is that in *The Shakespeare Apocrypha*, Ed. C.F. Tucker Brooke (Oxford: Clarendon Press, 1908; 1967).
10. My text for *The London Prodigall*, Ed. Tucker Brooke.
11. My text for *Volpone* is that in *English Renaissance Drama*, Eds. David Bevington, Lars Engle, Katharine Eisaman Maus, and Eric Rasmussen (New York: W.W. Norton and Co., 2002).
12. Park Honan, *Shakespeare: A Life* (Oxford: Oxford University Press, 1998), p. 335. He is quoting Frank Kermode, *The Sense of an Ending* (Oxford: Oxford University Press, 1967), p. 88.
13. Eamon Duffy, *The Stripping of the Altars: Traditional Religion in England c. 1400-1580* (New Haven: Yale University Press, 1992), pp. 355–56.
14. Quoted by E.A.J. Honigmann and Susan Brock in *Playhouse Wills, 1558-1642* (Manchester: Manchester University Press, 1993).
15. Peter Ackroyd, *Shakespeare the Biography* (New York: Nan A. Talese Doubleday, 2005), pp.19, 25, 92.
16. In the poem she refers to as "her WYLL and Testament" to the "famous Citie" of London, the ultimate poem in *A sweet nosegay or pleasant posye. Contayning a hundred and ten Phylosophicall flowers* (1573), Isabella Whitney wills the wealth of Cheapside with its gold and silver plate and threads, its fine fashions ("Hoods, Bungraces, Hats, or Caps,") and those at the Royal Exchange ("French Ruffes, high Purles, Gorgets, and Sleeves

of any kind of Lawne") to those able to purchase such goods, while she, now out of work, is forced to leave the city without any inheritance:

... though I nothing named have,
 to bury mee withal:
Consider that above the ground,
 annoyance bee I shall.
And let me have a shrowding Sheete
 to cover mee from shame:
And in oblivion bury mee
 and never more mee name
Ringings nor other Ceremonies,
 use you not for cost:
Nor at my burial, make no feast,
 your mony were but lost.

Her bitterness reinforces the inequality of property rights that Gerard de Narbon wishes to abrogate. My text is that edited by Betty Travitsky in *English Literary Renaissance* 18:1 (Winter 1988): 83–94.

17. Natasha Korda notes that "the tremendous popularity of [Swinburne's] treatise points to the increasingly diverse demand for [enumeration of classifiable goods]. Addressed to 'every subject of this realme, though hee bee but of meane capacity,' and written 'in our vulgar tongue' so that it 'may be understood of all,' his treatise went through two editions before Swinburne's death in 1623, and another eight posthumously." *Shakespeare's Domestic Economies*, p. 2.
18. The preceding material is drawn from Honigmann and Brock, pp. 11–15.
19. See Amy Louise Erickson, *Women and Property in Early Modern England* (London: Routledge, 1993), ch. 12, for a detailed discussion, with statistics, of women's wills.
20. Quoted by Davis, p. 229.
21. William O. Scott, "Contracts of Love and Affection: Lear, Old Age, and Kingship," *Shakespeare Survey* 65 (2002), pp. 36–37.
22. Mark Eccles, *Shakespeare in Warwickshire* (Madison: University of Wisconsin Press, 1961), p. 44.
23. Quoted by S. Schoenbaum, *William Shakespeare: A Documentary Life* (New York: Oxford University Press and Scolar Press, 1975), p. 246.
24. In an email of February 17, 2005; Sacks adds, "This is something that anyone working with last wills and testaments would begin to realize after reading the first dozen or so. One can therefore deduce nothing one way or other about a husband's feelings for his wife from the fact he left his wife his second best bed."

SHAKESPEARE'S LEGACY

1. Sir Walter Ralegh, *The Skeptic, or Speculation* (1651), p. 20.
2. Barbara Maria Stafford, "Levelling the Old Transcendence: Cognitive Coherence in the Era of Beyondness," *New Literary History* 35:2 (Spring 2004), p. 324.
3. Rebecca Goldstein, *Incompleteness: The Proof and Paradox of Kurt Gödel* (New York: W.W. Norton and Co., 2005), p. 163.
4. She is here paraphrasing the thought of Gödel.
5. Nicholas Wade, "Your Body Is Younger Than You Think," *New York Times*, August 2, 2005, "Science," p. 1.
6. John Carey, *What Good Are the Arts?* (London: Faber and Faber, 2005), p. 217, but see all of ch. 7.

BIBLIOGRAPHY

Aebischer, Pascale. *Shakespeare's Violated Bodies: Stage and Screen Performance*. Cambridge: Cambridge University Press, 2004.

Anonymous, "Arden of Faversham." In Arthur F. Kinney, Ed., *Renaissance Drama: An Anthology of Plays and Entertainments*, 2nd ed. Oxford: Blackwell Publishing, 2005.

——. "The Birth of Merlin." In Brooke, C.F. Tucker, Ed. *The Shakespeare Apocrypha*. Oxford: Clarendon Press, 1967.

——. "The First Part of the True and Honorable Historie, of the Life of Sir John Old-castle, The Good Lord Cobham." In Brooke, C.F. Tucker, Ed. *The Shakespeare Apocrypha*. Oxford: Clarendon Press, 1967.

——. "The London Prodigall." In Brooke, C.F. Tucker, Ed. *The Shakespeare Apocrypha*. Oxford: Clarendon Press, 1967.

——. "The Merry Devill of Edmonton." In Brooke, C.F. Tucker, Ed. *The Shakespeare Apocrypha*. Oxford: Clarendon Press, 1967.

——. "A Most Pleasant Comedie of Mucedorus." In Brooke, C.F. Tucker, Ed. *The Shakespeare Apocrypha*. Oxford: Clarendon Press, 1967.

——. "A Pleasant Commodie, of Faire [Em], the Millers Daughter." In Brooke, C.F. Tucker, Ed. *The Shakespeare Apocrypha*. Oxford: Clarendon Press, 1967.

——. "The Raigne of King Edward the Third." In Brooke, C.F. Tucker, Ed. *The Shakespeare Apocrypha*. Oxford: Clarendon Press, 1967.

——. "The Revenger's Tragedy." In Bevington, David, Lars Engle, Katharine Eisaman Maus and Eric Rasmussen, Eds. *English Renaissance Drama: A Norton Anthology*. New York: W. W. Norton and Co., 2002.

——. "A Yorkshire Tragedy." In Brooke, C.F. Tucker, Ed. *The Shakespeare Apocrypha*. Oxford: Clarendon Press, 1967.

Aquinas, Thomas. *Basic Writings*, Ed. Anton C. Pegis. 2 vols. New York: Random House, 1944.

Aristotle. "Metaphysics." In *The Basic Works of Aristotle*, Ed. Richard McKeon. New York: Random House, 1941.

——. "De Sensu and De Memoria" trans. G.R.T. Ross. Cambridge: Cambridge University Press, 1906.

Arnheim, Rudolf. *Art and Visual Perception: A Psychology of the Creative Eye.* Berkeley: University of California Press, 1971.

——. The *Power of the Center: A Study of Composition in the Visual Arts.* Berkeley: University of California Press, 1982.

——. "*Visual Thinking.* Berkeley: University of California Press, 1969.

Ashley, Leonard R.N. *Elizabethan Popular Culture.* Bowling Green. Ohio: Bowling Green State University Press, 1988.

Astington, John H. "Late Elizabethan Repertory and the Succession," unpublished paper.

Barker, Simon and Hilary Hinds, Eds. The *Routledge Anthology of Renaissance Drama.* London: Routledge, 2003.

Baxandall, Michael. *Painting and Experience in Fifteenth-Century Italy.* 2nd ed. Oxford: Oxford University Press, 1988.

Beaumont, Francis. "The Knight of the Burning Pestle." In Arthur F. Kinney, Ed., *Renaissance Drama: An Anthology of Plays and Entertainments*, 2nd ed. Oxford: Blackwell Publishing, 2005.

—— and John Fletcher. "The Maid's Tragedy." In Bevington, David, Lars Engle, Katharine Eisaman Maus and Eric Rasmussen, Eds., *English Renaissance Drama: A Norton Anthology.* New York: W.W. Norton and Co., 2002.

Berger, Ronald M. *The Most Necessary Luxuries: The Mercers' Company of Coventry, 1550-1680.* University Park: Pennsylvania State University Press, 1993.

Bevington, David. *Action Is Eloquence: Shakespeare's Language of Gesture.* Cambridge, Mass.: Harvard University Press, 1984.

——, Lars Engle, Katharine Eisaman Maus and Eric Rasmussen, Eds. *English Renaissance Drama: A Norton Anthology.* New York: W.W. Norton and Co., 2002.

Boethius. *The Consolation of Philosophy*, trans. W.W. Cooper. New York: Modern Library, 1943.

Bolam, Robyn. "Rewriting City Comedy through Time and Cultures: *The Taming of the Shrew*—Padua to London to Padua U.S." In Mehl, Dieter, Angela Stock and Anne-Julia Zwierlein, Eds., *Plotting Early Modern London: New Essays on Jacobean City Comedy.* Aldershot: Ashgate, 2004.

Bossy, John. *Christianity in the West 1400-1700.* Oxford: Oxford University Press, 1985.

Boswell, Jackson Campbell. "Shylock's Turquoise Ring," *Shakespeare Quarterly* 14:4 (Autumn 1963).

Brigden, Susan. *New Worlds, Lost Worlds: The Rule of the Tudors, 1485-1603.* New York: Viking, 2000.

Brooke, C.F. Tucker, Ed. *The Shakespeare Apocrypha.* Oxford: Clarendon Press, 1967.

Bruster, Douglas. "The Dramatic Life of Objects in the Early Modern Theatre"in Harris, Jonathan Gil and Natasha Korda, Eds., *Staged Properties in Early Modern English Drama.* Cambridge: Cambridge University Press, 2002.

——. *Quoting Shakespeare: Form and Culture in Early Modern Drama.* Lincoln: University of Nebraska Press, 2000.

—— and Robert Weimann. *Prologues to Shakespeare's Theatre: Performance and Liminality in Early Modern Drama.* London: Routledge, 2004.

Bouza, Fernando, *Communication, Knowledge, and Memory in Early Modern Spain,* trans. Sonia Lopez and Michael Agnew. Philadelphia: University of Pennsylvania Press, 2004.

Brown, John Russell. *Shakespeare Dancing: A Theatrical Study of the Plays.* Houndmills, Basingstoke: Palgrave, 2005.

Buck, A.R. "Cordelia's Estate: Women and the Law of Property from Shakespeare to Nahum Tate," in Wright, Nancy E., Margaret W. Ferguson, and A.R. Buck, Eds. *Women, Property and the Letters of the Law in Early Modern England.* Toronto: University of Toronto Press, 2004.

Bulman, James C. *The Merchant of Venice: Shakespeare in Performance.* Manchester: Manchester University Press, 1991.

Calderwood, James, *Shakespearean Metadrama.* Minneapolis: University of Minnesota Press, 1971.

Camden, Carroll. *The Elizabethan Woman.* New York: Elsevier Press, 1952.

Carter, Rita. *Mapping the Mind.* Berkeley: University of California Press, 1999.

Cary, Elizabeth. *The Tragedy of Miriam, the Fair Queen of Jewry* in Barker, Simon and Hilary Hinds, Eds. The *Routledge Anthology of Renaissance Drama.* London: Routledge, 2003.

Casati, Roberto. *The Shadow Club,* trans. Abigail Archer. New York: Alfred A. Knopf, 2003.

Chambers, E.K. *The Elizabethan Stage.* 4 vols. Oxford: Clarendon Press, 1923.

Chan, Mary and Nancy E. Wright. "Marriage, Identity, and the Pursuit of Property in Seventeenth-Century England: The Cases of Anne Clifford and Elizabeth Wiseman." In Wright, Nancy E., Margaret W. Ferguson, and A.R. Buck, Eds. *Women, Property and the Letters of the Law in Early Modern England.* Toronto: University of Toronto Press, 2004.

Christianson, David. *Timepieces: Masterpieces of Chronometry.* National Library of Canada: Quintet Publishing, 2002.

Clemen, Wolfgang, *A Commentary on Shakespeare's Richard III*, trans. Jean Bonheim. London: Methuen and Co., Ltd., 1957.

Corbin, Peter and Douglas Sedge, Eds. *Thomas of Woodstock, or King Richard the Second, Part One*," Manchester: Manchester University Press, 2002.

Cressy, David, *Birth, Marriage, and Death: Ritual, Religion, and the Life-Cycle in Tudor and Stuart England*. Oxford: Oxford University Press, 1997.

——. *Bonfires and Bells: National Memory and the Protestant Calendar in Elizabethan and Stuart England*. Berkeley: University of California Press, 1989.

Damasio, Antonio, *Looking for Spinoza: Joy, Sorrow, and the Feeling Brain*. New York: Harcourt, Inc., 2003.

Daniel, Samuel, *Selected Poetry and "A Defense of Rhyme,"* Eds. Geoffrey G. Hiller and Peter L. Groves. Asheville, NC: Pegasus, 1998.

Da Vinci, Leonardo, *The Notebooks of Leonardo da Vinci*, Ed. Edward MacCurdy. 2 vols. London: The Reprint Society, 1938, 1954.

Davis, Lloyd. "Women's Wills in Early Modern England." In Wright, Nancy E., Margaret W. Ferguson, and A.R. Buck, Eds. *Women, Property and the Letters of the Law in Early Modern England*. Toronto: University of Toronto Press, 2004.

Dekker, Thomas. "The Shoemakers' Holiday." In Arthur F. Kinney, Ed., *Renaissance Drama: An Anthology of Plays and Entertainments*, 2nd ed. Oxford: Blackwell Publishing, 2005.

——. John Ford, and William Rowley, *The Witch of Edmonton* , Ed. Arthur F. Kinney. London: A and C Black, 1998.

Dessen, Alan C., *Elizabethan Drama and the Viewer's Eye*. Chapel Hill: University of North Carolina Press, 1977.

——. and Leslie Thomson, *A Directory of Stage Directions in English Drama, 1580-1642*. Cambridge: Cambridge University Press, 1999.

Doebler, Bettie Anne. *"Rooted Sorrow": Dying in Early Modern England*. Madison: Fairleigh Dickinson University Press, 1994.

Dowling, John E., *Creating Mind: How the Brain Works*. New York: W.W. Norton and Co., 1998.

Drakakis, John. "'Fashion it thus'" *Julius Caesar* and the Politics of Theatrical Representation." In *New Casebooks: Julius Caesar*, Ed. Richard Wilson. Houndsmills, Basingstoke: Palgrave, 2002.

Draper, R.P. *The Winter's Tale: Text and Performance*. London: Macmillan, 1985.

Duffy, Eamon, *The Stripping of the Altars: Traditional Religion in England c. 1400-1580*. New Haven: Yale University Press, 1992.

Duncan-Jones, Katherine. "Did the Boy Shakespeare Kill Calves?" *Review of English Studies*, N.S. 55:29 (April 2004).

——. *Ungentle Shakespeare: Scenes from His Life*. London: Thomson Learning, 2001.

Eccles, Mark, *Shakespeare in Warwickshire.* Madison: University of Wisconsin Press, 1961.

Ekman, Paul and Richard J. Davidson, Eds., *The Nature of Emotion: Fundamental Questions.* Oxford: Oxford University Press, 1994.

Ellsworth, Phoebe C., "Levels of Thought and Levels of Emotion." In Ekman, Paul and Richard J. Davidson, Eds., *The Nature of Emotion: Fundamental Questions.* Oxford: Oxford University Press, 1994.

Engel, William E., *Death and Drama in Renaissance England: Shades of Memory.* Oxford: Oxford University Press, 2002.

Erickson, Amy Louise, *Women and Property in Early Modern England.* London: Routledge, 1993.

Evans, Joan, *English Posies and Posy Rings.* London; Oxford University Press, 1931.

Fletcher, John, *The Women's Prize, or The Tamer Tamed.* London: Nick Heron Books, 2003.

Foakes, R.A., *Shakespeare and Violence.* Cambridge: Cambridge University Press, 2003.

Folkerth, Wes, *The Sound of Shakespeare.* London: Routledge, 2002.

Ford, John. *'Tis Pity She's a Whore.* In Arthur F. Kinney, Ed., *Renaissance Drama: An Anthology of Plays and Entertainments*, 2nd ed. Oxford: Blackwell Publishing, 2005.

Frey, Charles H. "Man's Rage/Women's Grief: Engaging Death in *Titus Andronicus*," in *Re-Visions of Shakespeare: Essays in Honor of Robert Ornstein.* Newark: University of Delaware Press, 2004.

Frijda, Nico H., *The Emotions.* Cambridge: Cambridge University Press, 1986.

——. "Emotions Require Cognitions, Even If Simple Ones," in Ekman, Paul and Richard J. Davidson, Eds., *The Nature of Emotion: Fundamental Questions.* Oxford: Oxford University Press, 1994.

Garber, Marjorie B., *Dream in Shakespeare: From Metaphor to Metamorphosis.* New Haven: Yale University Press, 1974.

——. *Shakespeare After All.* New York: Pantheon, 2004.

——. *Shakespeare's Ghost Writers: Literature as Uncanny Causality.* New York and London: Methuen, 1987.

Garrard, William. *The arte of warre.* 1591.

Gazzaniga, Michael S. *The Mind's Past.* Berkeley: University of California Press, 1998.

Gilbert, Allan H. "The Wreath of Thorns in *Paradise Regained*," *Journal of the Warburg and Courtauld Institutes* 3:1/2 (October 1939-January 1940): 156–60.

Goldstein, Rebecca, *Incompleteness: The Proof and Paradox of Kurt Gödel.* New York: W.W. Norton and Co., 2005.

Green, Juana. "Properties of Marriage: Proprietary Conflict and the Calculus of Gender in *Epicone*." In Harris, Jonathan Gil and Natasha Korda, Eds., *Staged Properties in Early Modern English Drama*. Cambridge: Cambridge University Press, 2002.

Greenblatt, Stephen, *Hamlet in Purgatory*. Princeton; Princeton University Press, 2001.

——. *Shakespearean Negotiations*. Berkeley: University of California Press, 1988.

——. *Will in the World: How Shakespeare Became Shakespeare*. New York: W.W. Norton and Co., 2004.

Greene, Robert. *Friar Bacon and Friar Bungay*. In Bevington, David, Lars Engle, Katharine Eisaman Maus and Eric Rasmussen, Eds., *English Renaissance Drama: A Norton Anthology*. New York: W.W. Norton and Co., 2002.

Gross, John, *Shylock: A Legend and Its Legacy*. New York: Simon and Schuster, 1992.

Gross, Kenneth, *Shakespeare's Noise*. Chicago: University of Chicago Press, 2001.

Grote, David, *The Best Actors in the World: Shakespeare and His Acting Company*. Westport, Conn.: Greenwood Press, 2002.

Guilfoyle, Cherrell, *Shakespeare's Play Within Play: Medieval Imagery and Scenic Form in* Hamlet, Othello, *and* King Lear. Kalamazoo: Western Michigan University Medieval Institute Publications, 1990.

Gurr, Andrew. "Headgear as a Paralinguistic Signifier in *King Lear*," *Shakespeare Survey* 55 (2002).

——. "A New Theatre Historicism." In Peter Holland and Stephen Orgel, Eds., *From Script to Stage in Early Modern England*. Houndsmills, Basingstoke: Palgrave/Macmillan, 2004.

——. *The Shakespearean Stage, 1574-1642*. 3rd ed. Cambridge: Cambridge University Press, 2004.

Guy, John, *Queen of Scots; The True Life of Mary Stuart*. Boston: Houghton Mifflin Co., 2004.

Haddon, Celia. *The First Ever English Olimpick Games*. London: Hodder and Stoughton, 2004.

Hall, Edward. "The Union of the Two Noble and Illustrate Famelies of Lancastre and York (1548)." In *William Shakespeare, Richard III*, Ed. Anthony Hammond. London and New York: Methuen, 1981.

Harmon, A.G. *Eternal Bonds, True Contracts: Law and Nature in Shakespeare's Problem Plays*. Albany: State University of New York, 2004.

Harris, Jonathan Gil and Natasha Korda, Eds. *Staged Properties in Early Modern English Drama*. Cambridge: Cambridge University Press, 2002.

——. "Introduction: Towards a Materialist Account of Stage Properties,." In Harris, Jonathan Gil and Natasha Korda, Eds., *Staged Properties in Early Modern English Drama*. Cambridge: Cambridge University Press, 2002.

Hassel, R. Chris, Jr. *Songs of Death: Performance, Interpretation, and the Text of* Richard III. Lincoln: University of Nebraska Press, 1987. .

Hattaway, Michael. *Elizabethan Popular Theatre: Plays in Performance*. London: Routledge and Kegan Paul, 1982.

Heywood, Thomas. *A Woman Killed with Kindness*. In Arthur F. Kinney, Ed., *Renaissance Drama: An Anthology of Plays and Entertainments*, 2nd ed. Oxford: Blackwell Publishing, 2005.

Hill, Tracey. *Anthony Munday and Civic Culture: Theatre, History and Power in Early Modern London l580-1633*. Manchester: Manchester University Press, 2004.

Holderness, Graham. "'To Be Observed,' Cue One Macbeth." In *Re-Visions of Shakespeare: Essays in Honor of Robert Ornstein*. Newark: University of Delaware Press, 2004.

Holland, Peter, Ed. *Richard III*. New York and London: Penguin Group, 2000.

—— and Stephen Orgel, Eds. *From Script to Stage in Early Modern England*. Houndsmills, Basingstoke: Palgrave/Macmillan, 2004.

Holmer, Joan Ozark. *The Merchant of Venice: Choice, Hazard and Consequence*. New York: St. Martin's Press, 1995.

Homan, Sidney. *Directing Shakespeare: A Scholar Onstage*. Athens: Ohio University Press, 2004.

Honan, Park. *Shakespeare: A Life*. Oxford: Oxford University Press, 1998.

Honigmann, E.A.J. and Susan Brock, Eds. *Playhouse Wills 1558-1642*. Manchester: Manchester University Press, 1993.

Humphrey, Nicholas. *A History of the Mind*. New York: Simon and Schuster, 1992.

Johnson, David Martel. *How History Made the Mind: The Cultural Origins of Objective Thinking*. Chicago and LaSalle: Open Court, 2003.

Johnson, Steven. *Mind Wide Open: Your Brain and the Neuroscience of Everyday Life*. New York: Scribner, 2004.

Jones, Maria. *Shakespeare's Culture in Modern Performance*. Houndsmills, Basingstoke: Palgrave/Macmillan, 2003.

Jonson, Ben, *Bartholomew Fair*. In Arthur F. Kinney, Ed., *Renaissance Drama: An Anthology of Plays and Entertainments*, 2nd ed. Oxford: Blackwell Publishing, 2005.

——. *Epicoene, or The Silent Woman*. In Barker, Simon and Hilary Hinds, Eds. The *Routledge Anthology of Renaissance Drama*. London: Routledge, 2003.

——. Volpone. In Bevington, David, Lars Engle, Katharine Eisaman Maus and Eric Rasmussen, Eds., *English Renaissance Drama: A Norton Anthology*. New York: W.W. Norton and Co., 2002.

Jowett, John. "Introduction" to *William Shakespeare, Richard III*. Oxford: Oxford University Press, 2000.

Kemp, Martin, Ed. *Leonardo on Painting*. New Haven: Yale University Press, 1989.

——. *Leonardo*. Oxford: Oxford University Press, 2004.

Kerrigan, William, *Shakespeare's Promises*. Baltimore: The Johns Hopkins University Press, 1999.

Kidnie, Margaret Jane. "The Staging of Shakespeare's Drama in Print Editions." In *Textual Performances: The Modern Reproduction of Shakespeare's Drama*, Eds. Lukas Erne and M.J. Kidnie. Cambridge: Cambridge University Press, 2004.

Kiefer, Frederick. *Shakespeare's Visual Theatre: Staging the Personified Characters*. Cambridge: Cambridge University Press, 2003.

Kilroy, Gerard. "Requiem for a Prince: Rites of Memory in *Hamlet*." In *Theatre and Religion: Lancastrian Shakespeare*, Ed. Richard Dutton, Alison Findlay and Richard Wilson. Manchester: Manchester University Press, 2003.

King, John N. *Tudor Royal Iconography: Literature and Art in An Age of Religious Crisis*. Princeton: Princeton University Press, 1989.

King, T.J. *Shakespearean Staging 1599-1642*. Cambridge, Mass. Harvard University Press, 1971.

Kinney, Arthur F., *Faulkner's Narrative Poetics: Style as Vision*. Amherst: University of Massachusetts Press, 1978.

——. *"Lies Like Truth": Shakespeare,* Macbeth, *and the Cultural Moment*. Detroit: Wayne State University Press, 2001.

——. *Renaissance Drama: An Anthology of Plays and Entertainments*. 2nd ed. Oxford: Blackwell Publishing, 2005.

Ko, Yu Jin, *Mutability and Division on Shakespeare's Stage*. Newark: University of Delaware Press, 2004.

Koch, Christof, *The Quest for Consciousness: A Neurobiological Approach*. Englewood, Colorado: Roberts and Company, Publishers, 2004.

Korda, Natasha. *Shakespeare's Domestic Economies: Gender and Property in Early Modern England*. Philadelphia: University of Pennsylvania Press, 2002.

——. "Women's Theatrical Properties." In Harris, Jonathan Gil and Natasha Korda, Eds., *Staged Properties in Early Modern English Drama*. Cambridge: Cambridge University Press, 2002.

Kunz, George Frederick, *The Curious Lore of Precious Stones* (1913). New York: Dover Books, 1971.

Kyd, Thomas, *The Spanish Tragedy*. In Arthur F. Kinney, Ed., *Renaissance Drama: An Anthology of Plays and Entertainments*, 2nd ed. Oxford: Blackwell Publishing, 2005.

Lake, Peter with Michael Questier, *The Antichrist's Lewd Hat: Protestants, Papists, and Players in Post-Reformation England*. New Haven: Yale University Press, 2002.

Lasurence, Anne, *Women in England 1500-1700: A Social History*. New York: St. Martin's Press, 1994.

Ledoux, Joseph E. "Cognitive-Emotional Interactions in the Brain." In Ekman, Paul and Richard J. Davidson, Eds., *The Nature of Emotion: Fundamental Questions*. Oxford: Oxford University Press, 1994.

LeLoyer, Pierre, *A Treatise of Specters, Strange Sights, or Apparitions Appearing Sensibly vnto Men*, trans. L. Jones. 1605.

Levi, Peter, *The Life and Times of William Shakespeare*. New York: Wing Books, 1988.

Lockerd, Benjamin G., Jr., unpublished lecture notes.

Lopez, Jeremy, *Theatrical Convention and Audience Response in Early Modern Drama*. Cambridge: Cambridge University Press, 2003.

Luckyj, Christina. *"A Moving Rhetoricke": Gender and Silence in Early Modern England*. Manchester: Manchester University Press, 2002.

Lunney, Ruth, *Marlowe and the Popular Tradition: Innovations in the English Drama Before 1595*. Manchester: Manchester University Press, 2002.

Lyly, John, *Campaspe*, Ed. G.K. Hunter and David Bevington. Manchester: Manchester University Press, 1991.

——. *Sappho and Phao*, Ed. G.K. Hunter and David Bevington. Manchester: Manchester University Press, 1991.

McDonald, Russ, *The Bedford Companion to Shakespeare: An Introduction with Documents*. 2nd ed. Boston; New York: Bedford/St. Martin's Press, 2001.

Machiavelli, Nicolo, *The Prince*, trans. George Bull. Baltimore: Penguin Books, 1960, 1963.

Manley, Lawrence, Ed. *London in the Age of Shakespeare: An Anthology*. University Park: Pennsylvania State University Press, 1986.

Marlowe, Christopher, *The Complete Plays*, Ed. Mark Thornton Burnett. London: J.M. Dent, 1999.

——. *The Jew of Malta*. Ed. David Bevington. Manchester: Manchester University Press, 1997.

——. Tamburlaine the Great, Part I. In Bevington, David, Lars Engle, Katharine Eisaman Maus and Eric Rasmussen, Eds., *English Renaissance Drama: A Norton Anthology*. New York: W.W. Norton and Co., 2002.

——. "The Tragicall History of the Life and Death of Doctor Faustus." In Arthur F. Kinney, Ed., *Renaissance Drama: An Anthology of Plays and Entertainments*, 2nd ed. Oxford: Blackwell Publishing, 2005.

——. “The Troublesome Reign and Lamentable Death of Edward the Second.” In Arthur F. Kinney, Ed., *Renaissance Drama: An Anthology of Plays and Entertainments*, 2nd ed. Oxford: Blackwell Publishing, 2005.

Marston, John. “The Malcontent.” In Arthur F. Kinney, Ed., *Renaissance Drama: An Anthology of Plays and Entertainments*, 2nd ed. Oxford: Blackwell Publishing, 2005.

Massinger, Philip. “A New Way to Pay Old Debts” in Bevington, David, Lars Engle, Katharine Eisaman Maus and Eric Rasmussen, Eds., *English Renaissance Drama: A Norton Anthology*. New York: W.W. Norton and Co., 2002.

——. “*The Roman Actor*. London: Nick Hern Books, 2002.

Matthews, Paul M. and Jeffrey McQuain, *The Bard on the B*rain. New York: The Dana Press, 2003.

Maus, Katharine Eisaman, *Inwardness and Theater in the English Renaissance*. Chicago: University of Chicago Press, 1995.

Mazzotta, Giuseppe, *Cosmopoiesis: The Renaissance Experiment*. Toronto: University of Toronto Press, 2001.

Meagher, John C. *Pursuing Shakespeare's Dramaturgy: Some Contexts, Resources, and Strategies in His Playmaking*. Madison, NJ: Fairleigh Dickinson University Press, 2003.

Mehl, Dieter, Angela Stock and Anne-Julia Zwierlein, Eds., *Plotting Early Modern London: New Essays on Jacobean City Comedy*. Aldershot: Ashgate, 2004.

Middleton, Thomas. “A Chaste Maid in Cheapside” In Arthur F. Kinney, Ed., *Renaissance Drama: An Anthology of Plays and Entertainments*, 2nd ed. Oxford: Blackwell Publishing, 2005.)

M[iddleton], T[homas], *The Ghost of Lucrece*. 1600.

——. “Women Beware Women.” In Bevington, David, Lars Engle, Katharine Eisaman Maus and Eric Rasmussen, Eds., *English Renaissance Drama: A Norton Anthology*. New York: W.W. Norton and Co., 2002.

——. and Thomas Dekker, *The Roaring Girl* in Barker, Simon and Hilary Hinds, Eds. The *Routledge Anthology of Renaissance Drama*. London: Routledge, 2003.

—— and William Rowley. “The Changeling.” In Arthur F. Kinney, Ed., *Renaissance Drama: An Anthology of Plays and Entertainments*, 2nd ed. Oxford: Blackwell Publishing, 2005.

Morse, Ruth. ”What City, Friends, Is This?” In Mehl, Dieter, Angela Stock and Anne-Julia Zwierlein, Eds., *Plotting Early Modern London: New Essays on Jacobean City Comedy*. Aldershot: Ashgate, 2004.

Moseley, C.W.R.D., *William Shakespeare: Richard III*. “Penguin Critical Studies.” London: Penguin, 1989.

Munday, Anthony and Others, *Sir Thomas More*, Ed. Vittorio Gabrieli and Giorgio Melchiori. Manchester: Manchester University Press, 1990.

Nashe, Thomas. "The Terrors of the Night, or A Discourse of Apparitions (1594)." In *The Works of Thomas Nashe*, Ed. R.B. McKerrow. 4 vols. Oxford: Basil Blackwell, 1958.

Newman, Karen. *Fashioning Feminity and English Renaissance Drama*. Chicago: University of Chicago Press, 1991.

Nørrentranders, Tor, *The User Illusion: Cutting Consciousness Down to Size*, trans. Jonathan Sydenham. New York: Penguin Books, 1998.

Norris, Herbert, *Tudor Costume and Fashion*. Mineola, New York: Dover Publications, Inc., 1997.

Oatley, Keith. "Writing and Reading: The Future of Cognitive Poetics." In *Cognitive Poetics in Practice*, Ed. Joanne Gavins and Gerard Steen. London: Routledge, 2004.

Orgel, Stephen, *The Authentic Shakespeare: And Other Problems of the Early Modern Stage*. London: Routledge, 2002.

——. and Peter Holland, Eds., *From Script to Stage in Early Modern England*. Houndsmills, Basingstoke: Palgrave/Macmillan, 2004.

Orlin, Lena Cowen, *Elizabethan Households: An Anthology*. Washington, D.C.: The Folger Shakespeare Library, 1995.

——. *Private Matters and Public Culture in Post-Reformation England*. Ithaca: Cornell University Press, 1994.

Panek, Jennifer. *Widows and Suitors in Early Modern Comedy*. Cambridge: Cambridge University Press, 2004.

Parker, Patricia. "Temporal Gestation, Legal Contracts, and the Promissory Economies of *The Winter's Tale*." In Wright, Nancy E., Margaret W. Ferguson, and A.R. Buck, Eds. *Women, Property and the Letters of the Law in Early Modern England*. Toronto: University of Toronto Press, 2004.

Peck, Linda Levy. *Consuming Splendor*. Cambridge: Cambridge University Press, 2005.

Perkins, David. *The Eureka Effect: The Art and Logic of Breakthrough Thinking*. New York: W.W. Norton and Company, 2000.

Peters, Julie Stone, *Theatre of the Book 1480-1880: Print, Text, and Performance in Europe*. Oxford: Oxford University Press, 2000.

Phillips, James Emerson, Jr. "The Monarchic Cycle in *Julius Caesar* and *Anthony and Cleopatra*." In *Shakespeare's* Julius Caesar, Ed. Julian Markels. New York: Charles Scribner's Sons, 1961.

Picard, Liza, *Elizabeth's London: Everyday Life in Elizabethan London*. New York: St. Martin's Press, 2003.

Pinker, Steven, *How the Mind Works*. New York: W.W. Norton and Co., 1997.

Plutarch, *The Lives of the Noble Grecians and Romaines*, trans. Sir Thomas North, 1631.

Proctor, Thomas, *Of the Knowledge and Conducte of Warre*. 1578.

Puttenham, George. "The Arte of English Poesie (1589)." In *Sidney's* The Defence of Poesy *and Selected Renaissance Literary Criticism*. Ed. Colin Burrow. Harmondsworth: Penguin, 2004.

Pye, Christopher, *The Vanishing: Shakespeare, the Subject and Early Modern Culture*. Durham, N.C.: Duke University Press, 2000.

Ramachandran, V.S. and Sandra Blakeslee, *Phantoms in the Brain*. New York: HarperCollins Quill edition, 1999.

Ratney, John J., *A User's Guide to the Brain*. New York: Random House Vintage Books, 2002.

Rhodes, Neil, *Shakespeare and the Origins of English*. Oxford: Oxford University Press, 2004.

—— and Jonathan Sawday, Eds., *The Renaissance Computer: Knowledge Technology in the First Age of Print*. London: Routledge, 2000.

Richmond, Hugh MacRoe, *Shakespeare's Theatre: A Dictionary of His Stage Context*. London and New York: Continuum, 2000.

Ricoeur, Paul. *Memory, History, Epistemology*. Chicago: University of Chicago Press, 2004.

Riggs, David, *The World of Christopher Marlowe*. London: Faber and Faber, 2004.

Ripley, John, Julius Caesar *on Stage in England and America, 1599-1973*. Cambridge: Cambridge University Press, 1980.

Roberts, Sasha. "'Let me the curtains draw': The Dramatic and Symbolic Properties of the Bed in Shakespearean Tragedy" in Harris, Jonathan Gil and Natasha Korda, Eds., *Staged Properties in Early Modern English Drama*. Cambridge: Cambridge University Press, 2002.

Rogers, L.W., *The Ghosts in Shakespeare: A Study of the Occultism in the Shakespeare Plays*. n.d. n.p. 1949.

Rollins, Hyder E., Ed. *The Pack of Autolycus*. Cambridge,. Mass.: Harvard University Press, 1927.

Rossi, *Logic and the Art of Memory*, trans. Stephen Clucas. Chicago: University of Chicago Press, 2000.

Roth, Gerhard. "The Quest to Find Consciousness." In *Mind: A Special Edition of* Scientific American 14:1 (2004), pp. 32–39.

Rubenstein, Richard E., *Aristotle's Children: How Christians, Muslims, and Jews Rediscovered Ancient Wisdom and Illuminated the Dark Ages*. New York: Harcourt Inc., 2003.

Rymer, Thomas. *A Short View of Tragedy*. 1693.

S., W. "The Lamentable Tragedie of Locrine (1595)." In Brooke, C.F. Tucker, Ed. *The Shakespeare Apocrypha*. Oxford: Clarendon Press, 1967.

——. "The True Chronicle Historie of the Whole Life and Death of Thomas Lord Cromwell." In Brooke, C.F. Tucker, Ed. *The Shakespeare Apocrypha*. Oxford: Clarendon Press, 1967.

——. "The Puritaine; or the Widdow of Watling-Streete." In Brooke, C.F. Tucker, Ed. *The Shakespeare Apocrypha*. Oxford: Clarendon Press, 1967.

Sanders, Wilbur, *The Winter's Tale*. Boston: Twayne Publishers, 1987.

Sawday, Jonathan and Neil Rhodes, Eds., *The Renaissance Computer: Knowledge Technology in the First Age of Print*. London: Routledge, 2000.

Schank, Roger C. *Dynamic Memory Revisited*. Cambridge: Cambridge University Press, 1999.

Schanzer, Ernest, *The Problem Plays of Shakespeare*. London: Routledge and Kegan Paul, 1963.

Schoenbaum, S., *William Shakespeare: A Documentary Life*. New York: Oxford University Press and Scolar Press, 1975.

Schwyzer, Philip, *Literature, Nationalism and Memory in Early Modern England and Wales*. Cambridge: Cambridge University Press, 2004.

Scott, William O. "Contracts of Love and Affection: Lear, Old Age, and Kingship," *Shakespeare Survey* 55 (2002).

Shakespeare, William. *Julius Caesar*. Ed. Marvin Spevack. Cambridge: Cambridge University Press, 1988.

——. *Macbeth*. Ed. William C. Carroll. Boston: Bedford/St. Martin's Press, 1999.

——. *Measure for Measure*. Eds. Ivo Kamps and Karen Raber. Boston: Bedford/St. Martin's Press, 2004.

——. *The Merchant of Venice*. Ed. Charles Edelman. Cambridge: Cambridge University Press, 2002.

——. *The Riverside Shakespeare*, Eds. G. Blakemore Evans, Harry Levin, Herschel Baker, Anne Barton, Frank Kermode, Hallet Smith, and Marie Edel. Boston: Houghton Mifflin Company, 1974.

Shapiro, James. *A Year in the Life of William Shakespeare: 1599*. New York: Harper Collins 2005.

Sidney, Mary, Countess of Pembroke. *The Tragedy of Antony*. In Arthur F. Kinney, Ed., *Renaissance Drama: An Anthology of Plays and Entertainments*, 2nd ed. Oxford: Blackwell Publishing, 2005.

Smith, Bruce R., *The Acoustic World of Early Modern England*. Chicago: University of Chicago Press, 1999.

——. "E/loco/com/motion." In Holland, Peter and Stephen Orgel, Eds. *From Script to Stage in Early Modern England*. Houndsmills, Basingstoke: Palgrave/Macmillan, 2004.

Sokol, B.J. and Mary Sokol, *Shakespeare, Law, and Marriage*. Cambridge: Cambridge University Press, 2003.

Southworth, John, *Shakespeare The Player: A Life in the Theatre*. Phoenix Mill: Sutton Publishing, 2000.

Stafford, Barbara Maria. "'Leveling the Old Transcendence'": Cognitive Coherence in the Era of Beyondness," *New Literary History* 35:2 (Spring 2004).
Stern, Tiffany, *Making Shakespeare: From Stage to Page*. London: Routledge, 2004.
——. "Re-patching the Play,." In Holland, Peter and Stephen Orgel, Eds. *From Script to Stage in Early Modern England*. Houndsmills, Basingstoke: Palgrave/Macmillan, 2004.
Stockwell, Peter, *Cognitive Poetics: An Introduction*. London and New York: Routledge, 2002.
Stone, Lawrence, *The Crisis of the Aristocracy, 1558-1641*. Oxford: Clarendon Press, 1965.
Stubbs, Imogen, *We Happy Few*. London: Nick Hern Books, 2004.
Tamon, Miguel, *Friends of Interpretable Objects*. Cambridge, Mass.: Harvard University Press, 2001.
Teague, Frances, *Shakespeare's Speaking Properties*. Lewisburg: Bucknell University Press, 1991.
Thomas, Vivian, *Julius Caesar*. New York: Twayne Publishers, 1992.
Thomson, Leslie. "'With patient ears attend': *Romeo and Juliet* on the Elizabethan Stage," *Studies in Philology* (1995), 230-41.
Tilley, Morris P., *A Dictionary of the Proverbs in England in the Sixteenth and Seventeenth Centuries*. Ann Arbor: University of Michigan Press, 1950.
Todorov, Tzvetan, *Introduction to Poetics*, trans. Richard Howard. Minneapolis: University of Minnesota Press, 1981, 1982.
Travitsky, Betty "The 'Wyll and Testament' of Isabella Whitney" *English Literary Renaissance* 18:1 (Winter 1988).
Turner, John, *Macbeth*. Buckingham: Open University, 1992.
Webster, John, *The Duchess of Malfi*. In Arthur F. Kinney, Ed., *Renaissance Drama: An Anthology of Plays and Entertainments*, 2nd ed. Oxford: Blackwell Publishing, 2005.
——. *The White Devil*. In Bevington, David, Lars Engle, Katharine Eisaman Maus and Eric Rasmussen, Eds., *English Renaissance Drama: A Norton Anthology*. New York: W.W. Norton and Co., 2002.
Walker, Ralph, *A learned and profitable treatise of Gods providence*. 1608.
Williams, Penry, *The Later Tudors: England 1547-1603*. Oxford: Clarendon Press, 1995.
Wilson, J. Dover. *Lewes Lavater: Of Ghosts and Spirits Walking by Night* 1572.
Wilson, F.P., *The Plague in Shakespeare's London*. Oxford: Oxford University Press, 1927; 1963.
Wilson, Luke, *Theaters of Intention: Drama and the Law in Early Modern England*. Stanford: Stanford University Press, 2000.

Wilson, Richard, *Secret Shakespeare: Studies in Theatre, Religion, and Resistance*. Manchester: University of Manchester Press, 2004.

Wolfe, Jessica, *Humanism, Machinery, and Renaissance Literature*. Cambridge: Cambridge University Press, 2004.

Woolf, D.R., *Reading History in Early Modern England*. Cambridge: Cambridge University Press, 2000.

Wright, Nancy E., Margaret W. Ferguson, and A.R. Buck, Eds. *Women, Property and the Letters of the Law in Early Modern England*. Toronto: University of Toronto Press, 2004.

Yalom, Marilyn, *A History of the Wife*. New York: HarperCollins, 2001.

Zitner, Sheldon P., *All's Well That Ends Well*. Boston: Twayne Publishers, 1989.

INDEX

O

P

Q

R

S